Holy Restlessness

Holy Restlessness

Reflections on Faith and Learning

✦ ✦ ✦

PAUL J. DOVRE

🔲 AUGSBURG FORTRESS

Minneapolis

To all the saints, including my mentors
Carl Bailey, Nels Dovre, Joseph Knutson, Allwin Monson, and Ernest
Wrage

HOLY RESTLESSNESS
Reflections on Faith and Learning

Cover design: Joe Vaughan

Library of Congress Cataloging-in-Publication Data

Dovre, Paul John, 1935-
  Holy restlessness : reflections on faith and learning / Paul J. Dovre.
    p. cm.
  Includes bibliographical references.
  ISBN 978-0-8066-5771-4 (alk. paper)
  1. Faith—Sermons. 2. Lutheran Church—Sermons. 3. Concordia College (Moorhead, Minn.)—Presidents. I. Title.
  BV4637.D68 2009
  234'.23—dc22
                        2009020656

Manufactured in the U.S.A.
13 12 11 10 09 1 2 3 4 5 6 7 8 9 10

Contents

✤ Part One ✤

✤ Part Two ✤

✧ Part Three ✧

Foreword

There is a sense in which every college president is the spiritual leader of the campus. Most only realize that in times of crisis when it is clear that one voice must speak for the whole community and only one is in a position to reach across it to motivate, comfort, and heal. Some are better equipped for that role than others.

In colleges founded by religious communities, the expectation that the president will serve as spiritual leader was, until recently, the norm. The majority of those presidents were, in fact, ordained clergy or, in the case of Catholic schools, members of religious orders. However, in recent decades their numbers have declined precipitously, and the college presidency has become a more professionalized academic role, leaving open the question of whom, if anyone, provides spiritual leadership.

For Concordia College, our mission as a college is explicitly inseparable from our life as a Christian community. In his twenty-five years as Concordia's president, Paul J. Dovre served as the spiritual leader of the campus. Though he was the first non-ordained person to be elected president of Concordia College, he followed in the great tradition of clergy leaders at Norwegian-American Lutheran colleges. And he followed his predecessor Joseph Knutson's lead in stressing Lutheran religious identity at Concordia.

President Dovre's tenure coincided with a period of transformation in the church and in church college leadership. When the ELCA was formed with the merger of the ALC and LCA colleges, President Dovre wanted to ensure that Concordia would continue the traditional church-college ties it had always enjoyed.

It is to Dr. Dovre's credit that Concordia never distanced itself from its roots in the Lutheran confessions. He embraced the challenge of defining and reinforcing for its constituencies Concordia's commitment to its "great tradition"—the firm foundation of both the college and the church in the gospel. At the same time he negotiated changes in the "little traditions" borne of the folkways of the rural Norwegian Lutheran communities.

To this task, President Dovre brought his early studies in theology and his doctoral training in rhetorical theory and criticism, as well as his roots in the prairies of the Upper Midwest and in Concordia College. What he achieved as president was the development of Concordia into a modern liberal arts college, complete with shared governance systems that are taken for granted today. But more importantly, he brought his rhetorical gifts and his understanding of the rich complexity of Concordia's Lutheran heritage and its place at the center of college life to shape a community of scholars that still today understands and celebrates its identity as a college of the Lutheran church.

One of the most important ways that President Dovre accomplished this was through the homilies that he preached in daily chapel and for major college celebrations. Those homilies often spoke to the perceived needs of the college and its community at the time they were delivered. They drew on real experiences in the college community—from celebrations to sudden deaths—or his own experience growing up on the prairie as he modeled how the examined life was lived and how the dialogue of faith and reason enriched one's spiritual life. In doing so, he inspired generations of students and faculty to do likewise.

His homilies were meticulously crafted and contain messages that resonate with a range of listeners. They were written for scholars as well as college freshmen, but they always articulated Dr. Dovre's conception of the Lutheran identity of Concordia and reminded the community of its obligation to its tradition.

The title of this collection comes from a homily President Dovre delivered as part of the college's fall opening convocation the last year he served as president. In it he told the students (mostly new) that in addition to all their expectations that he thought would be fulfilled in their college years, he hoped that they would discover something they didn't expect—what he called "holy restlessness." He hoped that the questions, incongruities, and troubling encounters with differences, inequality, and suffering that they would encounter in their studies would, in combination with their faith development, lead them to hope and to conviction that would translate into action. This was a perfect expression of what his presidency was about. He was able to retain and even enrich the college's commitment to its Lutheran heritage by validating encounters with the richness of life and their contribution to the development of mature faith.

The messages in these homilies stand on their own. When read, as opposed to heard, they allow the reader to pause and appreciate the richness in them. But they are also inseparable from the messenger. To read the spare, thoughtful, inspired prose is to know the man behind them. As J.S. Bach inscribed the Reformation slogan, *Soli deo Gloria* (which is Concordia's motto) on his musical compositions, so has Paul J. Dovre inscribed it on his life.

Pamela Jolicoeur
President, Concordia College
Moorhead, Minnesota

Preface

This collection of homilies traces its origin to my call to the presidency of Concordia College in Moorhead, Minnesota, in 1974. Among the specifications in my letter of call was responsibility for the spiritual leadership of the college. Now, the spiritual leadership of a Lutheran college cannot and should not reside with one person—campus pastors, student religious organizations and their leaders, and ordained members of the faculty all carry either specified or generalized responsibility for nurturing the spiritual vitality of the college. And spiritual leadership is provided in more than one way. Leading, teaching, preaching, counseling, and singing are among the many ways in which this responsibility may be effected. But given my letter of call, I needed to determine how I was going to exercise spiritual leadership consistent with my gifts and experience.

In my teens and twenties I had given serious consideration to the ordained ministry. I had done a bit of preaching and spent a year at Luther Seminary in St. Paul, Minnesota, where I developed a life-long avocation in the study of theology. Thus, preaching in chapel, congregations, and other religious settings was not entirely new to me. I enjoyed the challenge of discovering a text and relating its lessons to a worshiping community. And as I went about my daily tasks with faculty and students, in the cafeteria or the senate meeting, on the athletic field or in the lecture hall, I was "reading" the hopes, fears, and questions of the campus audience. I was similarly engaged with the audience beyond the campus as a preacher in area congregations, as a participant in churchly meetings, and as a frequent member of various church task forces and committees. From the beginning of my presidency I would preach in chapel once a month, preach at Homecoming worship, and fill area church pulpits twelve or fifteen times a year. In addition, I led devotions for faculty and staff meetings all through my years as president. This collection of homilies is representative of those many occasions.

Lutherans have a multifaceted understanding of the Word of God. First, "Jesus Christ is the Word of God incarnate"; second, "the proclamation of God's message to us as both Law and Gospel is the Word of God"; and third, "the canonical scriptures of the Old and New Testaments are the Word of God" (chapter 2:02, *Constitution of the Evangelical Lutheran Church in America*). It is the second element that informs my understanding of the homilist's task, and my theological formation around the law-gospel paradigm has a strong influence on my preaching and leadership.

Luther's teachings on vocation are significant to me too. God loves us and promises us all the best. In thankfulness, we respond to God's call to love the neighbor, a love that is expressed in all the stations of our lives—home, church, career, and neighborhood. The comprehensiveness of this call touches the student seeking wisdom in a fallen world, the teacher seeking to discern the weight and meaning of new truths, the staff member who seeks to exercise his or her gifts in a complex organization, and the list goes on.

A third informing theological insight has to do with the paradoxical nature of reality. Luther's insights on this matter continue to shape religions in the modern era beginning with his insight that we are simultaneously saints redeemed by God in Christ and sinners incapable of our own redeeming. This insight is borne out in many life experiences where our calling is clear but its execution is filled with ambiguity and uncertainty. Yet we are called to serve God in such circumstances and we are able to do so because of the certainty of God's love. So my preaching has often addressed itself to the "faith and" issues where wonderment and uncertainty must be negotiated out of a careful understanding of both God's word and human circumstances.

The foregoing description of theological and confessional influences explains much about the subject matter and purpose of my homilies as well as the importance of knowing what was going on in the lives of students, faculty, and staff. One does a good deal of listening, reading, praying, and studying in the process of discerning the business that God is about in this world, the circumstances and aspirations of God's people, and the truth of the Word. The first section in this collection focuses on what the title of the book calls "faith and learning." Most of these "faith and" homilies address issues that were important to students—politics, freedom, discipline, vocation, suffering, truth. The second section addresses what I call the "seasons of faith." In this case, the seasons are both academic and liturgical. The final section addresses "elements of faith" and includes homilies on such matters as hope, grace, forgiveness.

These homilies span a goodly number of years, as the dates in the appendix indicate. Bringing what were originally spoken words to life in printed form is a challenge. I have done what I can. Now it is up to each reader to bring his or her own experiences and perspectives to bear on my work and help it breathe anew. In the task of selecting from among several hundred homilies, I have been encouraged by my wife Mardeth, my editor Susan Johnson, and many colleagues. And in all of this I have been inspired by students, by faith-filled friends, and by the Spirit of God. And always I pray, "May the words of my mouth and the meditations of our hearts be acceptable in thy sight, O Lord, our strength and our redeemer."
Amen

Paul J. Dovre, President Emeritus
Concordia College

PART ONE

Faith and Learning

What Does Faith Have to Do with It?

This collection begins with a selection of homilies directly framed by the subtitle of the book, *Faith and Learning*. That subtitle, in turn, is framed by Luther's view that faith life and life in the world are inseparable. Luther's continuing intellectual quest was consonant with St. Anselm's affirmation that "faith seeks understanding."

I recall how as a confirmation student and later as a college student I often pondered the question: "What does faith have to do with it?" The "it" varied. Sometimes it was a social issue, other times a personal choice or an academic query. But the question was always the same. And as a faculty member and college president I discovered that this core question transcends the generations.

Modern writers have helped us understand that our faith formation is evolutionary; that is, some questions are more important to us at one time than another. Furthermore, culture has a profound impact on how we discern this core question and how we answer it. The Lutheran understanding of vocation is that we are motivated to serve the neighbor and preserve the creation out of gratitude for

God's love. Acknowledging that calling is the first step; figuring out how to do it can be complicated because we are, according to Luther, *simul justus et pecator*—simultaneously saints and sinners. And the world in which we are called to carry out our vocations is more often colored gray than black and white.

So this first series of homilies addresses the question, "What does faith have to do with it?" in the context of a series of specific life experiences such as doubt, death, politics, discipleship, suffering, accountability, and other matters. They are offered in the hope that they might prompt the reader's reflection around some key issues in the Christian life.

Faith and Belief

2 Kings 2:1-12a; 2 Corinthians 3:12—4:6; Mark 9:2-9

When I was twelve years old our family took a trip to the mountains of Wyoming. I had read in geography books about the Big Horn Mountains rising out of the prairies to a height of over 9,000 feet, but to that point, the mountains were only a figment of my imagination. I remember that after we came in sight of them, it took another half-day's drive to actually arrive. But then, seeing was believing! On that same trip we went to Yellowstone National Park. I had of course read about Old Faithful and how it would send its 150-foot geyser skyward every sixty-five minutes—or so it was said. We arrived at the site and stayed for two performances of this wonder of nature, and again—seeing was believing!

The texts of this day are about seeing and believing, about the power of a vision of what is to be. Belief in such a vision can be life-changing, world-changing, and history-making. Visions are incredibly important. In *The Man of LaMancha*, Don Quixote sees in Aldonza not a lady of the street but a woman of refinement and character. "My Lady Dulcinea," he calls her. This vision changes Aldonza's perspective of herself so much that she is transformed. The change is so complete that near the end of the play when Sancho Panza speaks to Aldonza, she replies to him with quiet power, "My name is Dulcinea."

Last month we celebrated the birthday of Martin Luther King Jr. whose vision was articulated in three simple words: "I have a dream." It was a dream not for today but for tomorrow, a dream that would change the course of our history. Likewise, our gospel text from Mark is about seeing and believing, seeing and believing Christ triumphant, seeing in a way that transforms people from glory into glory. But before I hasten to the conclusion prematurely that seeing such a vision *is* believing, we must turn to a word from our text: seeing is *not* necessarily believing.

In Corinth, Paul found that many in the flock who had seen Jesus through the gospel Paul proclaimed had not believed the Christ to whom he pointed. According to Paul they could not really see Jesus because the Mosaic law in which they had been tutored from birth veiled their eyes. For them the Messiah they expected to see was one who would reclaim their political power and restore the rule of the judges. For them the kingdom of righteousness and glory was a place of human perfection where Mosaic law was observed in every particular. They could not "see" this Messiah who promised forgiveness to lawbreakers, love to homely people, and healing even to the unclean. So Paul said in sadness, "The god of this world has blinded the minds of the unbelievers" (2 Cor. 4:4). Seeing is not necessarily believing.

In our you-get-what-you-pay-for world, seeing the Christ is not necessarily believing his gospel. In a world that says you can be anything you want to be if you just have the right attitude and work at it hard enough—seeing the cross is not necessarily believing the grace. And for good, well-meaning Christian folk like most of us, it is a small step—a very small step indeed—to think that our acts of faithful worship and obedient service will gain us a couple of rungs on the ladder to spiritual glory.

There is a veil of another kind too. Dietrich Bonhoeffer spoke of it as cheap grace, the grace we confer on ourselves—no-cost grace. In Hubert Nelson's words, Bonhoeffer felt that the church of his day "doled out [grace] in generous quantities to whomever put their hands out, but it was essentially worthless [for] it could not resist the forces of evil. . . ."[1] With no sense of God's will, God's law, there is no need for repentance. And with no need for repentance, grace is superfluous and empty of the power of persuasion. Our modern day tendency to rewrite the law into gospel is an insidious expression of a very old tendency. Seeing is not necessarily believing.

Peter, James, and John gave us yet another illustration of the axiom. In the gospel text from Mark 9, we read how they accompanied Jesus to the mountain of transfiguration. There they saw Jesus transfigured before their very eyes. And the first thing Peter thought of was, "Let's build something to commemorate this! Let's fix this moment in time." According to Mark, Peter was so frightened he didn't know what he was saying. That may be so, but even in rational, cool-headed moments of absolutely startling inspiration, folks have been prompted to say, "Let's remember this. Let's build a statue." In fact, we do it frequently for matters of remarkably little significance. As individuals we are tempted to freeze in time our religious experience: Confirmation was so wonderful that we want to hold our religious education right there, or The Bethel Bible series was so great that now we know all that we can be expected to know about the scriptures.

And as a church it is also tempting to either stop the clock or try to turn it back. The neighborhood around us changes, but we want to stay with our historic constituency. The musical style of the culture changes, but we don't want any variation on Bach, Brahms, or Christiansen. The social gospel that has dominated our church agendas for the past two decades has been unmasked as wanting, but it is easier to stay with it in the face of the uncomfortable mandates of law and gospel that lie at the heart of the evangelical tradition. With clear eyes we see that the gospel changes things. It moves the church and transforms individuals and renews communities. The gospel is a change agent. While we may try to build monuments to the gospel, we will never be able to build a monument to its power, for that is a moveable feast. So one word from our lessons today is that seeing is *not* believing when veils cover our eyes or when we try to freeze the gospel in time.

Another word for the day tells us when seeing *is* believing. Paul wrote in his second letter to the Corinthians that seeing is believing when one turns to God. Then, as Paul put it, we are transformed from glory into glory and the light shines in our darkness. Under what circumstances can this happen? While God may choose any circumstances, we have God's assurance that he comes to us when we are in worship. Worship is the occasion where God's people surround us, where God's Word is laid open, where the means of grace are shared. This place of worship is, after all, where believers are inspired by God's Spirit who works the miracle of faith whereby seeing is believing!

God comes to us in worship. And God will come to us when we are listening. The great lesson from earlier this season about Samuel always touches me. When God called Samuel in the night, it took until the fourth try before the young boy realized that God was talking to him. At that point he listened and the world changed. Seeing was believing. God comes to us when we listen.

God comes to us when we persist. In our Old Testament lesson (2 Kings 2:1-12), we read how Elisha stayed the course with Elijah; he followed him over the rough spots when others fell away. As a result, he saw Elijah's transfiguration and God named him the successor prophet of all of Israel. Persistence, sheer persistence. Jesus' disciples Peter, James, and John could be described as terrified, doubting, petty infighters. But our Gospel text also shows they were persistent in following Jesus, and at his ascension they saw it all and they believed. Their ministries would shape the world in the years thereafter. And our dear father in the faith, Martin Luther—never quite able to settle in his mind the words from Romans about "grace alone," never quite able to reconcile those with the indulgence selling church—persisted and saw God's light. Seeing was believing, and the church experienced a reformation that continues still. God comes to us when we persist.

God comes to us in all of these and other circumstances of his choosing. And then the Spirit moves us in ways we might never have imagined, just as it moved our forebearers to build churches, colleges, and seminaries. Today the Spirit moves us to acts of compassion among the sick, the homeless, and the disconsolate. It moves us to face the seemingly overwhelming obstacles of a thoroughly secular culture. It moves us out of ghetto churches and into the rainbow culture that surrounds us. It moves us out of smug judgment to compassionate empathy. And it moves us out of the gospel to the daily bread of forgiveness and discipleship.

When God comes to us in such places and circumstances, then "seeing is believing" and Don Quixote's Aldonza becomes Lady Dulcinea, Martin Luther King's dream becomes a reality, and your life becomes a flowing river of grace.

Amen

Faith and Community

Genesis 21:22-27

Nearly every year for the past twenty-four I have devoted one chapel service to a discussion of community. I have done so, in part, because of the name and traditions of this place called Concordia. Our name was selected in the wee hours of the morning on April 15, 1891, by three pioneer pastors. When we celebrated our centennial a few years ago, several of the descendants of those pioneers participated in the event. *Concordia* means "the goodness of harmony"—or literally, "hearts together, working in unison." The history and life of this college reflect the tradition implied by our name. We work hard at community here. Consensus, listening, and collegiality characterize both the structures and substance of our common life.

Many images of community have been helpful to us at Concordia over the years. One not very helpful image has been that of the "happy Cobber," which is most often intended as a caricature rather than as a description of community. Other more helpful images include the one the apostle Paul used in his letter to the Corinthians when he described the many parts of the body—or community—united by a common spirit (see 1 Corinthians 12). It is the image of the "connected community." In his letter to the Ephesians Paul talked about speaking the truth in love, about saying helpful words, the kind that build up (Eph. 4:15-16). It is an image of the "civil" or "affirming" community.

Another image is contained in the biblical text—the image of the covenant community. Let me explore this concept and some of its implications for our life together. We understand a covenant to be a promise, a commitment from one person to another. The root of the idea of covenant is found in the Old Testament, where God made a covenant with the Israelites, promising, "I will be their God and they shall be my people" (Jer. 31:33). God promised them a land of their own, a place of plenty and freedom, of justice, integrity, hospitality, and wholeness.

But God wasn't the only one making covenants. God's people did too. They made covenants with each other, and the story of Abraham and Abimelech is a beautiful example (see Gen. 20: 1-18; 21:22-34). The mighty Abimelech had wronged Abraham by taking from him his wife, Sarah. God confronted him with his sin so Abimelech sought Abraham's forgiveness. In addition to returning Sarah, he sent along sheep and oxen and slaves and said, "My land is before you; settle where it pleases you" (Gen 20:15). Later, when Abraham confronted Abimelech about a problem concerning a well, Abimelech made things right. Abraham was grateful and gracious and, we are told, the two made a covenant. The place they made the covenant was Beer-sheba—"by the well." In observance of their covenant it would be a place of community, of peaceful gathering and refreshment. In that way community was a product of their covenant.

The idea of covenant has been part of our faith tradition, kept alive for centuries, sometimes misused but never replaced. Jesus identified with it, and Paul announced that he and his follows were ministers of the new covenant in Christ. But what's involved in taking covenant as a source of meaning and direction for our lives? What are the marks of a "covenant community?" First there is commitment to each other. Theologian Martin Buber said that in turning to each other, we turn to God. Covenant people are committed to others. And, in our case here at Concordia College, there is not only commitment to each other but also commitment to the world we are called to serve.

The people in a covenant community are also committed to values. The values God taught the Israelites—peace, justice, hospitality, honor, integrity, charity, orderliness—divine ordinances delivered at Sinai and passed along by the great rabbis, prophets, and priests have not really been improved upon. But within covenant communities those value commitments are active rather than passive. Let me illustrate: I believe a covenant community is not content with mere acceptance of others, of people who look and speak and act in different ways. Acceptance does not necessarily stop us from excluding people. We tend to divide ourselves according to interest, ability, or belief—the liberals hang out together, as do the jocks and the musicians. And cliques can result in a quiet, unspoken exclusiveness. A covenant community, on the other hand, is inclusive. Its members reach out to the one who is different, the one whose historic standing has been compromised by intention or tradition. Differences in race or sex or ability or interest are not permitted to exclude anyone.

Similarly, a covenant community is not content with openness, commendable though that may be. I was part of a state commission that met last week. It is composed of church workers, attorneys, politicians, business people, educators, and students. We were open with each other and it was a feast! But covenant people go from openness to interdependence. The needs of the homeless, for example, will require more than openness to data and analysis by a variety of experts—those needs require the collaboration of scholar, practitioner, developer, politician, and neighbor. Until this interdependence is realized, the needs of the homeless will be less than adequately addressed.

Covenant people are not content with tolerance either; they move on to justice. In the '60s we passed civil rights laws and raised the consciousness of Americans. Everyone is for tolerance these days. But that does not mean the absence of bigotry and prejudice, does it? The evidence of racial distrust, homophobia, and intercultural animosity tells us that tolerance is not enough. Justice must be the agenda—the proactive work of people to insure that all are dealt with justly, that poor people have access to a better life, that women are treated with equality, that all children have an equal chance to survive and succeed—those ends are not the product of tolerance but of justice.

I also don't believe a covenant community is content with diversity; rather, it presses toward unity. Diversity is a gift. It brings vitality to our persons and to our community. Yet without losing those gifts of diversity, we seek unity. Unity in spirit and value is the glue that brings people of many colors and classes and causes and creeds together. The community that pursues unity takes risks. In the words of author and educator Parker Palmer, such communities are "less like utopia than like a crucible or a refiner's fire." In the pursuit of unity, God wants us to learn something about ourselves, about our limits and our need for others. Parker reminds us that "community means the collision of egos, and while there is the pain of not getting our way, there is the promise of finding the Way."[1]

Another mark of a covenant community is that it is collaborative, not individualistic. I believe this has some special significance for an academic community. We stress individual growth, individual goals, individual performance, and the academic model may easily mimic the economic model that stresses completion. Well, we are not a better place or a better people when someone fails to "get the idea" or "solve the problem" or "parse the verb" or "complete the paper" or "pass the exam." We are a better place when everyone succeeds; that's what this community strives for. Professors are not the only teachers, and students are not the only learners; it's a collaborative process and it's what co-inquiry is all about. Parker Palmer put it this way: "Community will constantly remind us that our grip on truth is fragile and incomplete, that we need many ears to hear the fullness of God's word."[2] I believe that in a covenant community leadership is not equated with power but with service. The ways of the world are too often the ways of Machiavelli, where leadership is understood in terms of power and intrigue. But under the sign of the cross, leadership is transformed from mastery to service, from confrontation to conversation, from control to compassion. So it was for Abraham and Abimelech, and—God willing—so may it also be for us.

Undergirding it all is grace. Grace was God's motive in making a covenant with Israel. Grace was the impulse that led to the covenant of reconciliation between Abraham and Abimelech. Grace was the impulse for Christ's new covenant. Life in community is a gift of grace for each of us as we are forgiven and forgiving, sometimes picking up the pieces, always building and rebuilding our covenants. Community is a byproduct of all of this: the commitments, the values, the grace, and the action.

Abraham gave sheep and oxen to Abimelech on the occasion of their reconciliation. A tree was planted by a well at Beer-sheba and a place of community was created to mark what they had done. That community was a byproduct of the grace they had received and their covenant with each other. And so, too, is this "hearts together" place.

Amen

Faith and Complaint

Psalm 13; Matthew 27:46

"Be all that you can be" goes the recruiting slogan. It is a slogan fully in tune with the spirit of the age—that you and I are in control, that we can make things happen. We have fix-it-yourself car manuals and therapies for almost every aggravation of mind, body, and spirit, and if you can follow the directions, you are supposed to be able to record your favorite television program three weeks in advance!

The eminent theologian George Marsden makes the argument that in an earlier age ours was a God-centered society and all of life was understood in religious terms. But now we have become a human-centered universe in which the center of attention is our needs and our technological capacity to make ourselves comfortable and successful. Yes, even some contemporary theology tends to make of God one who will respond to the human will instead of vice versa. So we can become positive thinkers and God will go along.

In this context, a psalm of lament such as Psalm 13, a complaint against God, seems really out of place. I mean, with God all is supposed to go well. Blaming God when things go wrong is, well, wrong-headed theology. So we say, in the rush of a bad mood or bad luck, I will pray when I feel better. This problem-solving, positive-thinking God doesn't want to hear from me right now. But David didn't know any better. Listen to what he said: "How long, O Lord? Will you forget me forever? How long will you hide your face from me? How long must I bear pain in my soul, and have sorrow in my heart all day long? How long shall my enemy be exulted over me?" (Ps. 13:1-2).

What shall we make of David's complaint? And what shall our be-all-that-we-can-be generation make of Jesus' complaint on the cross, "My God, my God, why have you forsaken me" (Matt. 27:46)? Or his plea in the garden, "Let this cup pass from me" (Matt. 26:39)? Were these just bad prayers reflecting a lack of confidence, or do they reveal a clue to God's grace?

I thought of this text in the context of a recent event, the death of a Cobber, the father of another Cobber, in a plane crash last week. The sky was clear, the pilot was competent—"all he could be," I assume—but they crashed a mile after takeoff and all hands on board were killed. When I spoke with his widow, she was full of lament and unanswerable questions. Hardly a day goes by in your life and mine or within our community without the lament of a friend or a stranger stricken by death, injustice, or misfortune.

So what do we make of the lament of David of ages past, of the widow of just days past or of the friend or stranger of the present moment? The first thing we can take from this psalm of lament is that we can tell our troubles to God. God is interested. God cares. We can even complain to God. We are not sure what was troubling Israel, the voice of this psalm. Maybe it was a financial loss or defeat in battle; maybe it was a famine or religious strife—of which there was always plenty. We don't know the cause but we know the people were hard-pressed, the end seemed near, and as is usually the case, some in the community were gloating over the difficulties of others. This is a prayer of complaint; the psalmist is clearly angry that God seems indifferent to their situation. Likewise, Jesus had lived a full and obedient life in service to the one he called Father, and there we see him on the cross complaining, "My God, my God why have you forsaken me?"

We too can identify with the problems that give rise to prayers such as these, for we all experience pain and sorrow some time in our lives. It may come with the betrayal of a friendship or the death of one too young or too dear to die or the loss of a crop to elements of wind and weather. There is a lot we don't understand and find hard to accept about experiences like these. But one of the revealed truths of this psalm is that we can complain to God. God would rather hear from us than have us carry our anger around all bottled up inside, intent on our own meager solutions.

A second message we can take from this psalm is that faith in God is not the cure-all for all that ails us. God is Lord of all; we cannot take the power away from God. God is not to be mocked or manipulated by our actions, by our will. Note that the psalm did not report a set of happy results. Indeed, we know that even though God was the very center of the Israelite's lives, this nation still seemed to move from one crisis to the next. And Jesus' cry on the cross did not result in the Roman soldiers taking down the cross and saying, "We made a mistake, Jesus, you are free to go." And Paul's tormentors did not desist nor was his thorn in the flesh removed.

We cannot expect God to be our bandage or full coverage rescuer either. James L. Mays, professor emeritus of Hebrew and the Old Testament at Union Theological Seminary, says that this psalm strips away the illusion of faith as a cure, an escape, a panacea for fear and anxiety. We can't expect that all wars will cease because God blesses the peacemakers, or that temptation will disappear because we confess God as Lord, or that enemies will become friends because we are gracious to them, or that plane crashes or cancer or catastrophic illness or self-indulgence will cease to destroy precious lives. No, it is really more likely to go the other way—to the cross. After all, that is why Christ came and why his cross is still among us, because there are still burdens to be borne and sins to be put to death.

Well, you say, this is certainly depressing stuff. It's nice to know that God will listen but it's too bad that God can't just fix things. And that brings us to the nub of it all, the central message of this psalm, that our suffering, our complaint, our lamentation, which God is willing to hear can be an occasion for grace. The psalmist was moved to that kind of conclusion: "But I trusted in your steadfast love; my heart shall rejoice in your salvation. I will sing to the Lord, because he has dealt bountifully with me" (Ps. 13:5-6).

We don't know in a rational way how the psalmist moved from complaint to praise. There is no evidence in the psalm or the history of Israel or the life of Christ or the history of the church or the experience of the widow that the causes of the complaints were removed. If none of that happens, then what? Well, the good news on this day is that even in the worst of times, God transcends! God doesn't avoid the cross; God deals with it. The psalmist and Jesus and the apostles all testify that God's grace transcends the cross—even though the terror might not leave us. God didn't spare Jesus the agony, but God saved him. Luther, in speaking of the mood of this psalm, described it as the "state in which hope despairs and yet despair hopes at the same time."

And for Paul the suffering and the lamentation was not removed, but there was grace and it allowed him to say, "For I am convinced that neither death, nor life, nor angels, nor rulers, nor things present, nor things to come, nor powers, nor height, nor depth, nor anything else in all creation, will be able to separate us from the love of God in Christ Jesus our Lord" (Rom. 8:38-39).

Each of us knows about that hope that transcends the darkness; it may have been a death in our family, it may have been a business crisis or a broken relationship, but somehow we were sustained and on the other side of our lament we gave thanks to God. Lamentation and suffering are not consistent states of life, thanks be to God for that. But such experiences come to all of us, and in this psalm and in the words of Jesus on the cross, we all know that we have a God who will hear us—our anger and our complaints. And we have a God who will be with us in those times, a God who has promised to transcend the travail. It is that triumph that lets us sing God's praise in the midst of tears and in the face of death itself. Our hope is built on nothing less.

Amen

Faith and Death

Psalm 90:12; 1 Peter 1:24-25

This message is framed by four events over the past four months. In November I was scheduled to be a guest preacher at Good Shepherd Lutheran Church in Helena, Montana. I was looking forward to a reunion with a number of Cobbers who lived in the area. When I arrived, I discovered that one of them was approaching the end of a difficulty pregnancy. The weekend I was there she gave birth, prematurely, to twins. One died shortly after birth and the other within a few days.

Death has also come to our college family here. In the last days of December the call came from Tara's roommate that Tara had died in a car-truck accident on a winter night. And last week the call came early in the morning—Brian was dead in a traffic accident and Carl was injured in stable but serious condition. The next day came news of the death of longtime friend of this place, Alma Wije in Eventide Nursing Home at the age of 102.

Last Tuesday night after visiting Carl's family and then Brian's, I found my theme for today in a song for all seasons: "Teach us to count our days that we may gain a wise heart" (Ps. 90:12). Whether death comes at the age of four hours or in the prime of life or the fullness of time—our hearts and minds yearn for wisdom. We yearn for wisdom about death. As the reference from Psalm 90 makes clear, our days are numbered. We are not, after all, invincible—miracles of science, safety air bags, condoms, life support systems, and healthy lifestyles to the contrary notwithstanding.

In earlier verses of the same chapter, the psalmist speaks about the transitory nature of life in words that echo these profound phrases from the book of Isaiah: "All people are grass, their constancy is like the flower of the field. The grass withers, the flower fades . . . surely the people are grass" (Isa. 40:6-7). As sure as the sun rises day after day, the flower will eventually fade and the grass that produced it will brown and die. We live in a dying world—the soil beneath us will continue to wear away, these buildings will fall, and our bodies will one day fail us. Death is certain. There is no escape at age four days or twenty-two years or five score plus two. Lord, teach us to count our days that we may gain a wise heart about death.

And teach us to count our days so that we may gain a wise heart about God's love for us. In their quest for wisdom, people often ask at a time like this, "Did God want those premature infants or our contemporaries Tara and Brian or the college's good friend Alma to die? When this bad thing happened to these good people was God manipulating the universe, bringing his holy judgment to earth? Not the God I know! The God I know gives us life and permits us to live in freedom and at risk. The God I know wept when Jesus died on the cross. The God I know wept with you and me when our beloved Tara and Brian were taken from us. And yes, the God I know has welcomed them home just as our parents welcome us home from a long journey—except that God's homecoming is beyond our comprehension.

In a reprise of the Old Testament reference, the apostle Peter wrote: "For 'All flesh is like grass and all its glory like the flower of grass. The grass withers and the flower falls, but the word of the Lord endures forever.' That word is the good news that was announced to you" (1 Peter 1:24-25). The good news never sounds better than in the face of the unexpected, cataclysmic, sudden, and violent death. And the good news is that "neither death, nor life, nor angels, nor rulers, nor things present, nor things to come, nor powers, nor height, nor depth, nor anything else in all creation, will be able to separate us from the love of God in Christ Jesus our Lord" (Rom. 8:38-39).

The good news of God's absolutely unqualified love transcends the fading flower and the dying grass of life; it comprehends the cataclysmic, unexpected, and sometimes violent end of time. Lord, teach us to count our days that we may gain a wise heart about your love for us.

And teach us to count our days that we may gain a wise heart about your will for us. As Cobber basketball forward Pete Balmer said last Thursday morning, "A bad day or a bad game takes on a whole different meaning in the face of death." Death puts our values, our life choices, and yes, our bad days, in a whole new perspective. In the verses following this text from 1 Peter, there is good news for the living. Peter's message was that, having received the good word—the redeeming word—our lives will change. His counsel is concrete: "Rid yourself, therefore, of all malice, and all guile, insincerity, envy, and all slander . . . abstain from the desires of the flesh that wage war against your soul" (1 Peter 2: 1, 11). For "you are a chosen race, a royal priesthood, a holy nation, God's own people, in order that you may proclaim the mighty acts of him who called you out of darkness into his marvelous light" (1 Peter 2:9).

It is not unusual that people who confront death begin to count their days and then discover new wisdom about life. I saw it in a friend when the death of someone close to him helped him gain new wisdom about stewardship. I saw it in my grandfather when my grandmother died; it was the turning point in his struggle with alcoholism. I have experienced similar "turnings" in my life on more than one occasion of death and tragedy. So don't shrink from the wisdom about daily living that may come on such occasions, for surely God speaks to us in such events.

Such new wisdom underscores the mission of this college. We are each given time and occasion to serve God when we work with our colleagues and classmates, when we serve in our churches and our communities, when we volunteer for Habitat for Humanity or the Dorothy Day House. And we have occasion to serve God in the moral judgments we make each day, whether in the public transactions of the community or in the private transactions of our individual lives. Each action, each decision matters. It is an occasion for service, an opportunity to bear witness to the hope and righteousness that God has given to us.

You have heard the story of Tara and Brian, stories of people whom we loved. We don't know how they counted their days but we know that their hearts were wise—wise in faith, wise in service. So too was my octogenarian friend Alma Wije. She and her husband had no children, so they adopted all of us out of gratitude and love. So God, teach us to count our days so that we too may gain a wise heart.

Amen

Faith and Discipleship

Psalm 100; Jeremiah 23:1-8; Matthew 20:17-28

Have you ever asked someone else to do a job you were afraid to do? Of course you have. We all have. I recall our son as a child always asking his mother to do it first—whether it was skiing a new mountain slope in the winter or testing the swimmibility of Bad Medicine Lake in the early summer.

James and John may have asked their mother to intervene with Jesus on their behalf because they were afraid. Of course the stakes were much different. They were seeking a position in the kingdom Jesus had been speaking about for several months. This wasn't about a ski slop or cold water—but about their life's calling. And, as we see in this text from Matthew 20, Jesus answered their question. He literally took them to school on that question and several others. Indeed, this text has a good deal of applicability to anyone who is sorting or resorting his or her discipleship. Let me discuss a few of the lessons I find in this text.

The first lesson is that discipleship involves making a choice. I am not speaking here of decision theology—the view that faith is an act of our volition—for we confess that faith is a gift of God's Spirit. What I am talking about are all the decisions that disciples make once they have received that gift and accepted the mantle of discipleship. In the first verses of the reading we hear how Jesus foretold his coming crucifixion. Now, Jesus the human being had some options you might say. He was, after all, a pretty good teacher and might have gotten tenure had he returned to the Temple school in Galilee where his ratings were very high. But Jesus, Son of God, listened to

God's call and chose to submit himself to the humiliation, the pain, the abandonment, and the death that was to come.

Discipleship always involves a choice—a decision to respond to the grace and call of God by worshiping God, by loving the neighbor and caring for creation. The call may be fulfilled in many different ways—but it involves a decision to do so. The twelve were called by Jesus and, we are told, they chose—they decided to follow him. And throughout their discipleship they faced many decisions, some of them very difficult.

Another lesson from this text is that we may be confused about our discipleship. The Old Testament text from Jeremiah is a classic example of this. All the kings Jeremiah was condemning had been called to rule over a kingdom originally ordained by God. But the rulers failed to understand the obligations of their office. They were supposed to rule with justice, caring for the homeless, the orphans, and widows, and showing mercy to the lowly. Instead, they accumulated possessions and friends for their own prestige, comfort, and advancement. And God's judgment on their conduct of office could not have been clearer.

James and John didn't get it either. They wanted to be on the right and left hand of Jesus in his kingdom, but they were imagining a kingdom with political power and economic influence. But Jesus, we recall, talked about the first being last and the last first, about becoming a slave to others—it was leadership as insurgency. He mentioned the traditional expectations of leaders by name and then said, "It will not be so among you" (Matt. 20:26). There would be a whole new agenda in his kingdom—James and John were taken to school indeed.

Let's talk about another challenge for disciples—the problem of overconfidence. Even after Jesus explained to James and John what leadership was about in his kingdom, they said, "We are able" (Matt. 20:22). They didn't understand their false confidence. They didn't anticipate the cowardice they would exhibit at Jesus' end nor did they imagine martyrdom at their own ending. "We are able" has been the post Renaissance rallying cry. But in spite of the wonders of health and science, of technology and human wisdom, there are loud signals of our overconfidence on every hand. Consider the current state of our economy and our overconfidence in prosperity. Or look at the impasse in Iraq or the scourge of Aids and Alzheimer's. Look at global hunger, where in spite of the Green Revolution, 30,000 children will die today of hunger, disease, and other consequences of poverty. Consider the maldistribution of the world's wealth where the wealthiest 500 people have the same income as the world's poorest 416 million.

In our confidence we forget human miscalculation, we forget human limitation, we forget the resourcefulness of the old Adam. We're still looking for magic apples in the garden to feed our indulgence. And even when we remember the realities of Adam, we may assume that, like James and John, we can take on any task. But then faced with the realities of the task, we demur. As Lord Tennyson wrote—we aspire to rule, but have no wish to live "in that fierce light which beats upon a throne."[1]

Perhaps one of the most common experiences of disciples is discovering the ambiguity of our task. I think of all the students I have known who have lacked clarity about their discipleship. Which major should I choose? Which job? Which career? Which venue of service? We vary greatly in talent, in inclination, and in personality—the disciples surely did and so do we. And while God calls us to service, the details are usually left to us. God probably figured that with our intelligence and the good counsel of others, we would figure out the details. I like what C. S. Lewis said about the matter: "The scene and the general outline of the story is fixed by the author, but certain minor details are left for the actors to improvise."[2]

I spent a number of years trying to sort out my calling. I was not as bright as others—somewhat above average but not in the top rank, at least not until late in the game. Finally, I took stock of my inclinations and such gifts as I had and set course. And the rest has been a series of surprises—a full and fulfilling vocation indeed. I learned in the course of things to accept the ambiguity, to trust my gifts and the counsel of others, and to follow the inclinations that I prayed God had placed in my life.

Another source of ambiguity comes in the form of questions without obvious or easy answers. Faith isn't a fix. There is, for example, the oxymoron of servant leadership. How can one be both servant and leader? What about the juxtaposition of power and humility? Or the necessity of wealth to do good and "selling all one has?" I leave it to you to add to the list—the point is, discipling is full of paradox as Jesus made clear to James and John.

All of which leads to a final question: Where is the "I will be with you always" God in all of this? Where is God in the midst of the paradoxes, the confusion, the misplaced confidence, and the ambiguities? I believe that God is with us in the Word—in texts like those this day. In the Word, God teaches us through parables, stories, and ethical reflections about love and justice, about charity and faithfulness, about righteousness and honor—in short, about my discipleship. It is there, in scripture, and if we are serious about our discipleship it calls for our faithful attention.

And the "I will be with you always" God is present in the people around us—in the friend who listens to your indecision and anxiety with patience and understanding, in the neighbor who calls you to account for misplaced confidence and unfaithful discipleship, in the faculty mentor who helps you sort through an understanding of your gifts, talents, and calling, and in the experience of a summer job or a campus activity where you discover the matching of duty and delight, of gift and passion. The "I will be with you always" God is there when you call to him in prayers of confession or praise, prayers of confusion or resolution.

James and John discovered that God was with them in their arrogance and ignorance, in their confession and confusion—God saw them all the way home. Yes, God walks with his disciples, so go and serve!

Amen

Faith and Doubt

John 20:24-29

Imagine if you will a group of long distance runners comparing notes. One tells about his hip pointer, another discusses the blisters on her heel, the third talks about his shin splints, the fourth describes chronic knee problems, and still another details the pain of her pulled hamstring. All the while another young runner is in the corner feeling left out and somehow inadequate because she has never had an injury. We would of course tell that young athlete that, thank God, shin splints and pulled hamstrings are neither inevitable nor prerequisite to distance running.

I would begin with the same words about life and faith. The nature of the race, of growth in life and faith, is not the same for all. Some are born with a kind of grace and loveliness that enables them to come to new challenges with strength and openness and to depart from them with confidence and composure, while others experience doubt and anger and anxiety and other forms of personal trauma. I feel it's important to say that from the top lest some conclude that they, like the athlete in my story, feel that they are missing something because they lack the equivalent of a pulled "faith string." Praise God, we are not all alike and it is not required that all will struggle according to some common definition. Praise God, too, that when struggles arise we can depend on God to be there. Consider how Jesus respected and responded to people who experienced struggle and doubt in their faith life. Recall his extensive give and take with the priests in the synagogues and the scribes and Pharisees in the street. And especially remember his respectful regard for his disciple Thomas in his hour of doubt. In other words, Jesus is not surprised by doubt and he will care for us in such times.

According to Georgetown University president, Timothy Healy, when a young mind and a great work or idea come into conflict, the result can be chaotic and explosive. And so it may be whether it is contact with the riddles of Macbeth or the categories of Marx or the strange logic of Jesus. Let me describe two struggles in my faith life that bear out Healey's prediction: one was my struggle with vocation and the other with intellectual doubt. As a student I was concerned about making the right choice of a career. My hometown pastor and some teachers encouraged me to enter the ministry. But I liked farming, having been taught by a wise and progressive farmer father. I set out for college without a clear career goal but with the possibility of the ordained ministry always on the edge of my thinking. During college years other possibilities emerged as I encountered new ideas and new mentors. Law, business, and teaching all seemed like interesting options.

But I was still deliberating about the idea of preparing for the ordained ministry. There were still people encouraging me in that direction, and yet I was confused and uncertain because I had been led to believe that one must have a clear and certain call to enter the ministry, a call which I had not experienced. I talked to people about it, prayed about it a good deal, and even spent a year in a seminary in what eventually turned out to be a struggle that lasted several years.

Through my odyssey, by the intercession of friends and God's Spirit, I came to understand and claim for myself the Lutheran understanding of vocation. Ministers, I discovered, don't always wear clerical collars—they also wear overalls and coveralls, uniforms and dresses, suits and gowns. I came to understand and claim that ministry is really defined by the use of our gifts in serving our neighbors, acting as agents of God's reconciling love. So I became a teacher and my career has changed a time or two since that early struggle, but my vocation—my calling—has not. So I counsel you: don't expect to be called by a bolt of lightening or a dream in the night. Rather, let your gifts, your interests, the counsel of your mentors and the influence of God's Spirit lead you, and if that leads you into ordained ministry, praise God for that. But if it leads you to another form of ministry, praise God for that too.

Now to my struggle with intellectual doubt. Graduate school was a foreign environment to me in the late '50s and early '60s. For the first time I was working and studying with people who did not share Christian presuppositions, although they were good, bright, and likeable people. The measure of truth in graduate school was the method of science and the rules of induction. Whether we studied the rhetoric of Aristotle or St. Augustine, the history of colonial America or Korzybsky's philosophy of language and reality—the role of religious experience was frequently called into question and discounted. I was challenged as never before to give reason—to myself and to others—for the hope that was in me. I was challenged to wrestle with intellectual doubts as to the meaning, the pragmatic ground for my religious beliefs. I was challenged to explain how an organization with such great ideals as the church could act—or fail to act—so hypocritically. And on the eve of the civil rights movement, that was not easy to explain. I struggled over books and coffee cups, with atheist and agnostic friends, with a gifted pastor friend and with my wife who was always full of grace and patience.

I did not come out of that struggle with a set of answers to all the questions and for all time. But I came to understand more clearly the nature of the church as an instrument made holy by God's intention and by Word and sacrament and not by the perfection of its ministry. The church does not always live up to its principles any more than this college is always a caring community—but God's grace is always present and therein lies the essence of the church, of our faith and of this community. And I came to understand more clearly the nature of faith. Whether in politics or religion, science or philosophy—faith is a level of trust in presuppositions that, in the final analysis, are unseen. We live our lives based on such presuppositions. As a Christian, I believe that Christ is the most profound presupposition, and I see evidence of this presupposition in life just as surely as the scientist verifies molecular theory in the laboratory. That struggle with intellectual doubt strengthened my faith. For those who enjoy life in the world of ideas, the dialectic between the Christian faith and culture produces challenge, the kind of challenge that can spur growth in vocation and faith. And if what you believe matters, you can't always keep readjusting it to the passing parade of intellectual thought, lest your beliefs—and your deepest self—lose the quality of integrity and merely twist in the wind.

In the struggles that I have described perhaps the most important experience I had was the experience of grace, God's acceptance of me in the midst of my wanderings and wonderings. God was with me. That is the bedrock, the essence of my faith, immovable and unchanging. These have not been my only struggles, and I assume that there are more to come. I also do not claim that my experience will be yours or that it provides answers to your needs. To end where I began, I don't recommend that everyone have themselves a struggle over vocation or intellectual doubt. But if you do, don't be afraid. For the steadfast, immovable and "fear not" God will be with you. And you can count on that.

Amen

Faith and Honor

Ephesians 6:1-4

Today I want to talk about the fourth commandment, the one we learned on our parent's knee or in our Sunday school teacher's class: "Honor thy father and thy mother." I have chosen this topic for a number of reasons. First, we do not often speak about it. Second, for students, vacation is only a few weeks back, time most of you spent with your parents. I have had a chance in my work to watch the changing relationships between parents and children through the college years. And you either have or will notice that each time you return home after an absence, your relationship with your parents changes. You still love them and they still love you—that's the same. But other things are changing. You're not as dependent on them as you once were or maybe your ideas have changed. You may notice that your relationship, while still strong and vibrant, is in some ways different, and you may wonder what to make of that in terms of this, the "honor" commandment.

The other reason I was drawn to this commandment is personal. A few months ago I lost my last parent. That has changed the circumstances of my life and has led me to ponder my role as a parent to my children and, I suppose, as a mentor to other parents.

Well, that's a whole load of hay and I've only twelve minutes, so let's go. Let's consider first the significance of this commandment. It comes in fourth position in the Decalogue, just after the three commandments about our relationship with God. The next seven commandments all have to do with our relationship to others, and this commandment about our relationship to our parents stands first in that sequence. This points to the primacy of family relationships in the sight of God and in the reality of our lives. We get some idea of the importance of parents in the ministry of Jesus. According to the Gospels, Jesus' family seemed to be around on many occasions. Jesus saw the relationship as a binding one, and even in his extremity on the cross, he cared for his mother. But the Judeo-Christian tradition is not the only tradition to understand the primacy of the parental relationship. In fact, both Plato and Aristotle spoke of honor for parents in the same breath as honor for the gods.

The significance of this commandment is indicated in one more way. As the text reads, honoring parents is the key to our own wellness as children: "Honor your father and mother . . . that it may be well with you and you may live long on the earth" (Eph. 6:2-3). But according to Paul the relationship is reciprocal, in that the wellness of children is a responsibility of parents: "Do not provoke your children to anger" (Eph. 6:4), he said, as a way of counseling parents about a healthy family.

So this fourth commandment is significant to us in a number of ways. But what does it mean to honor our parents? In the Small Catechism Luther wrote that it means "we should fear and love God, and so we should not despise our parents and superiors, nor provoke them to anger, but honor, serve, obey, love, and esteem them."[1] I believe that what Luther was telling us in his explanation is that the genesis of our relationship with our parents begins with our relationship to God. The gospel news of creation and reconciliation changes us and stirs in us love and gratitude. This commandment helps us give expression to that love in our relationship to our parents. Honoring and obeying begins with love for God and then love for parents who, in the words of children's author, Robert Munsch, "love you forever" and "like you for always."[2]

But the sweet harmony of life is not the only song in our family repertoires. There is also the song of sin, of anger, of deceit, of disrespect, of disapproval. Some theologians call it "original sin" and others "the old Adam." But whatever its name, it is destructive of relationships between us and God and among family members. We recall that the commandment was originally given to Moses and the Israelites on a wilderness journey filled with temptations and difficulties as well as manna and deliverance. So God gave this commandment as a gift to enable families to both express their love and to hold in check their destructive tendencies.

"Well and good," you say. "We love God and we love our parents and honor them too but what about when parents are out of line?" The tradition clearly acknowledges that possibility. Paul admonished parents not to provoke their children to anger. And we remember that when Jesus was in the temple listening to the elders he came into conflict with his parents' expectations. Jesus put people on notice that he was to have priority—priority to the point that it might set family members against one another (see Luke 12:51-53). Perhaps that's what was behind Paul's words that children should "obey your parents in the Lord" (Eph. 6:1). Christ is to have priority in our relationships, and if a parent leads us in ways contrary to Christ's path, then we are free to disobey. In extremity, the commandment does not mean slavish submission to immoral authority. "Obey your parent in the Lord, for this is right" is Paul's good counsel and it surely applies to such increasingly common circumstances as family abuse and neglect. Those are circumstances where children need the protection and support of other authorities—teachers and police and judges and pastors. May God spare us from such circumstances, but, once in them, may we find the courage and support necessary to sustain a righteous disobedience.

There is another possible ambiguity about living out this commandment that does not have to do with immoral or oppressive parents but with the more frequent and more subtle pressures of life in the family. You come home from college with a new idea, maybe about politics or—perish the thought—about religion. You try out your new idea on Mom or Dad. They get nervous, maybe defensive. In my student days at Concordia, President Joseph Knutson gave a chapel talk just before the first break of the year. He would predict the kind of generational clash that might occur when we launched our new-found wisdom on our parents. He urged us to be thoughtful, respectful, and to remember that Mom and Dad weren't so dumb! My father and I had some remarkable battles about politics in my student days. I wasn't always very understanding in some of those discussions—nor was he. But thanks be to God, we experienced grace. The tie did not end—neither then nor now.

Family trials are not inevitable but neither are they to be unexpected. It may be a clash over politics or ethics, over friends or career choices, over lifestyle or marriage choices, over religious preference or practice. In such circumstances—some of which are unavoidable—the commitment to love and honor is all the more important. Honor becomes a significant discipline and love a significant grace, both of which must be carefully tended. And when one hears the expression that blood runs thicker than water, it is sometimes a sign of the presence of both the discipline and the grace that prevents disagreements from dividing parents and children. And so the tie never ends.

In all of these experiences of being a child and parent, we are sustained by the love of God who creates and cares, admonishes and encourages. Our parents, in turn, are primary channels of God's love for us. And the good news is that no matter what the circumstance, God never ceases to be our parent and, by divine grace, the love of our mothers and fathers never abandons us. Even in death the spirit of this love lives on in us. So "honor your father and mother . . . that it may be well with you and you may live long on the earth."

Amen

Faith and Legacy

1 Corinthians 8:1-13

The story Paul tells us about the people in Corinth is certainly of historical interest. He was writing to them about the problems of first century Christians. The Corinthians were people with brief experience in the Christian faith, people living amidst all kinds of religions, gods, and demons. Paul had lived and preached among these people and they had been touched by God's Spirit. Paul's time with them had been a time of exuberance, celebration, and high hopes. But at the time of this letter, things had changed dramatically and the people of Corinth were trying to figure out how to live out their faith on "the morning after" as it were.

The question of the day was, "Can we eat meat?" Why in the world would Paul bother to mention an issue like that in a letter? Perhaps it made sense in the first century but surely the editors of the epistle in preparing the Bible for publication would have had enough sense to edit out an issue of such seemingly minor consequence. Or was there some good reason to include this story? Could there be some remote implication for us?

Before we address these questions perhaps we should ask who these people, these Corinthians, were anyway? While most of them were brand new to Christianity, they were not brand new to religion. In earlier days they had worshiped other gods. Some worshiped the gods of nature—the moon and the stars. They read the signs of the solar system and their scripture consisted of the sayings of the astrologers. Others worshiped animals; dogs and cows or camels were thought to contain the spirits of their ancestors. Some worshiped fertility, or the mystery of procreation, at a time when life was short and infant mortality was high. Sacrifice was a part of each of these religions, sometimes including human sacrifice, with young children laid on an altar and killed. Other sacrifices are less offensive to our senses, like the meat of animals, which is the subject of this text. Finally some of the people worshiped the intellect. They were called Hellenists, a well-educated people who devoted their lives to the discovery of truth.

It was to this mixed band that Paul wrote his letter, a letter devoted ostensibly to eating meat. And Paul had unique messages to the different people in his audience. To the people who had worshiped the gods of nature in the past, the astral deities and fertility gods, his message was one of understanding. He knew those people who had discovered a new life in Christ still lived in the shadow of their old life. They had, in many cases, grown up thinking it was wrong to eat meat that had first been offered to idols. Their consciences and characters had been formed on that basis. Paul understood that they would never live fully outside of that influence so he said, in effect, "I understand. And I think we all had better respect your experience and your sensitivities to the old gods."

Paul had another message for the intellectuals and the rationalists. They thought that they had it all figured out. For them the gospel of Christ meant that they could eat anything they chose and so, no doubt, they did. Further, they figured that a matter like the efficacy of eating meat first offered to idols could and should be treated rationally. That was all there was to it! So, they thought, "Those other folks are really backward, out-of-it people." And there is reason to believe that they lorded their wisdom over their colleagues in the faith and probably made life very miserable for them. It was not just their intellectual intimidation, mind you; it was their act of eating the meat, an act that compromised the new life in Christ for many of the initiates in the faith.

This is an interesting first century story you say, but what does it say to us? I mean, eating meat offered to idols is no longer an issue.

Or is it? As people in Christ we don't escape the legacies of our past. If we grew up thinking of God as an authoritarian parent, we may not entirely escape the feelings of guilt and doubt. If we grew up in a home with lots of dos and don'ts, we may not be at ease with the freedom to act in a certain way, and we note in ourselves a tendency for too much food, too much drink, too much gossip, too many things. Being in Christ doesn't take us out of the world; we don't escape those tendencies. As such, our actions may be harmful both to ourselves and—through our witness—to others.

Some people grew up with what a friend of mine used to describe as a "spiritual bellyache." That is, they grew up with a certain narrow conception of God and religious faithfulness and then discovered it was really different, but they never stopped rebelling against their former understanding. Such is the power of habit and belief. Like those Corinthians who found a new life in Christ but still had to deal with the residue of the old life, we too may discover that we can't escape all the demons and former gods in our lives. As people in Christ we may misplace confidence in our intellectual understanding, just as some did in Corinth. Paul had two messages for the intelligentsia in Corinth: "First, don't expect new understanding to blot out years and generations of established attitudes and practice. And second, don't assume that your intellectual insight somehow puts you in a special, exclusive, and elite category over against others in the faith." Now, we believe in the importance of intellectual understanding. We are committed to that as a college and as individual learners. And we study religion because we believe that growth in understanding and growth in faith go hand in hand. But it is tempting to assume that intellectual understanding is the same thing as faith. We believe that if we can just get the head part right, the heart part will follow. And it is equally tempting to use our intellectual understanding of religious tradition as a kind of club.

As a "good" Lutheran boy who understood the concept of justification by grace through faith, I used to laugh at my Catholic classmates who were diligent about not eating meat on Fridays. That was, in my view, an unnecessary discipline, and one certainly not required by God. As an outstanding confirmation student I understood that baptism was efficacious whether total or partial, as an infant or an adult, and so we Lutheran kids laughed at the Baptist kids with their total immersion baptism for adults only. And it is tempting, really tempting, for successful students of 100- or 400-level religion courses to lord it over those who still think of the four Gospels as having been the work of only four writers, or those who believe that Luther or Calvin or Aquinas were saints without blemish, or those who take seriously the gift of glossolallia or speaking in tongues, or those who don't appreciate or practice the richness of the formal liturgy. It is as tempting for us as it was for some of those people in Corinth to become proud and self-righteous about our intellectual understanding.

And as people in Christ, we too can become stumbling blocks to those still living in the shadow of demons. Paul talked about eating meat in the presence of those who had a religious problem with it. "Under those conditions," he said, "you are sinning against Christ." I cringe at this counsel for in countless ways I am not a good example. I cause people to stumble in more ways than I know about. I say, "So let me off the hook, Lord. Let me do my earnest best and let everyone else do their earnest best and may grace see all of us through." But there is sharpness in Paul's counsel and it comes to people like you and me, well-informed believers. I look at the world just beyond my bifocals and discover that there are alcoholics who can't abide a small libation, dependent persons who need the community of the clean, physically abused individuals who recoil from a well-intentioned hug, friendless souls who will do virtually anything in exchange for something that passes for affection, and insecure people who will respond to almost any suggestion and anxious ones who mistake silence for rejection. I can become a stumbling block to any of these people.

In the face of God's will and Paul's counsel we are led, first of all, to our knees to confess the times and ways we cause people to stumble, whether through stiff-necked intellectualizing of the faith or overconfidence in our ability to escape the effects of demons in our lives or by the frequency with which we become stumbling blocks for others. In all of these and like matters, I am led to my knees in confession of sin. And in this realization of my own predicament, I am led to forgive others who have, and do, bring me to crisis moments in my faith.

And finally, in fear and trembling, I am led to ask the God of Mary Magdalene and Paul and the Corinthians—the God who redeems people—to redeem me, to grant me humility in my wisdom, respect for the demons of the world, and diligence in my witness to others.

Amen

Faith and Politics

Philippians 4:8-9; Ephesians 4:25-32

The election just past was a busy one for several Concordia graduates. Among them were seven in our region who were campaigning for legislative or statewide office. Four of the seven were victorious and two of those who lost, lost to other Cobbers. This may be an argument for some artful re-districting in the future.

Most feel it is good to have the election behind us. There is widespread cynicism about buying elections, about empty promises. And there is disgust at so-called negative politics. The lead headline from Fargo columnist John Sundvor's election eve story in *The Forum* read: "Ten thousand lakes can't clean up one of America's dirtiest races." Many share his view so there are cries for reform in campaign financing and campaign practices.

Where do we go from here, that is, "we" as Concordia people? Our mission statement makes it clear that we are to influence the world, and if that is so, it means involvement in the public square of political life.[1] Most of the decisions that we would like to shape— decisions about the use of resources, about public safety and education, about care for those in need, about the mission of our congregation, about the quality and direction of our academic program or life in our residence hall corridor—will involve some measure of political activity.

The inevitability about political activity in our lives leads to a second question: What does our faith tradition have to say to the Christian in the public square? First of all, the Christian tradition can shape our attitude toward the public square. Politics deals in probabilities, not absolutes. Aristotle, representing a pre-Christian tradition but a tradition familiar to people like the apostle Paul, taught us that. It was the whole premise of his rhetoric: people need a way to argue respectfully, rationally, and effectively in arriving at proximate solutions to sometimes unclear propositions. Politics is about human issues and its premises and results are often imperfect and incomplete. Theologian Reinhold Niebuhr in his landmark work, *Moral Man and Immoral Society*, was concerned about the naiveté of some religious idealists in the public square who forgot "the egoism of the human spirit."[2] Politics, he said, is the area "where conscience and power meet, where the ethical and coercive factors of human life will interpenetrate and work out their tentative and uneasy compromises."[3] Politics is the place where we are to be involved in working for the common good. Luther argued for that by urging Christians to join with others, believers or not, in discerning the just and helpful act.

In addition to shaping our attitudes, the Christian tradition can shape how we view the goals of life in the public square. Paul had that in mind when he addressed the citizens of Philippi with these words: "Whatever is true, whatever is honorable, whatever is just, whatever is pure, whatever is pleasing, whatever is commendable, if there is any excellence and if there is anything worthy of praise, think about these things" (Phil. 4:8). Philippi was a place of some diversity. And we believe that Paul respected the work of the philosophers and priests and judges of that community who, though not Christians, were serious about matters of goodness and honor and justice. He said to his friends, in effect, if there are ideas that are good and true and just in other traditions, claim them.

Another key insight from the Pauline tradition is the emphasis on unity as a political end. Paul dealt with a good deal of difference and disagreement among the people with whom he ministered. But he always urged people to transcend those differences by claiming the common ground of the gospel, by recognizing the interdependence of diverse people with diverse gifts. "Build up the body" was his frequent slogan. Indeed, reconciliation was one of the most powerful motifs of Paul's work as he dealt with communities in which diversity was experienced as more of a problem than an opportunity. Remember his letter to the Corinthians in which he acknowledges the differences among the people—some thought of themselves as followers of Paul, others of Cephus, others of Apollos, and still others of Christ (see 1 Cor. 1:10-17). Paul urged these people to be united in the same mind and in the same purpose.

In these brief illustrations we discover that our tradition can shape our view of political ends in rather profound ways. And it can shape our vision of political means as well. A central issue is how we deal with political differences, with conflict, in the public square. One of the most obvious insights we can gain from reading the letters of Paul is that we ought to air out our differences. The early Christians had rather profound differences of opinion about the role of the Jewish tradition in the Christian community, and the parties to that conflict gathered together in Jerusalem to hash things out. Obviously, they believed there would be merit in airing their disagreements. Or, again, one thinks of almost every one of Paul's letters to the Christian communities that he had established. Up front Paul acknowledged the problems faced by those communities: problems of disunity, problems of slackness in the Christian life, problems of doctrine. Paul didn't pull any punches about these matters, and we might assume these occasions of difference may have become occasions for new and creative solutions.

Another of Paul's most profound injunctions for our understanding of political means is contained in this verse from Ephesians: "So then, putting away falsehood, let all of us speak the truth to our neighbors, for we are members of one another" (Eph. 4:25). Speak the truth, and speak it in love. I recall a homily by campus pastor Phil Holtan on the fifth petition of the Lord's Prayer: "Forgive us our trespasses, as we forgive those who trespass against us." Pastor Holtan shared the text in which Jesus said that if someone has wronged you, you should take it up with that person one on one. If the one who has offended you does not respond, then take another with you and if that doesn't work, still one more and if that doesn't work, then tell the assembly. This is, I submit, a formula for speaking the truth in love—not to embarrass or harm or offend or win—but trying to deal with the other in truth and with love.

The premise behind Paul's advice about telling the truth in a loving way is that we are neighbors, we are members one of another. There is an inseparable relationship between how we speak to our neighbor and the health of our neighborhood, and perhaps it is not too much of a leap to say that there is a profound relationship between our political conduct and the character of our community. Paul has more advice for us in his suggestion that we avoid harmful words. He urges us to let no evil talk come from our mouths, to put away wrath and anger and slander and malice. It is in our nature for many of us to deal with disagreements in a disagreeable way. It is tempting, for example, to attack people rather than the arguments they present. We call this "argument *ad hominem*" and we saw plenty of it in the recent election. It is also very tempting to put people into categories and ignore the quality of their argument—categories such as liberal, conservative, athlete, theater major, student, administrator, and the list goes on. And most of us probably prefer to listen to only one side of an argument, the side that to us is politically or socially or theologically correct. Each of these practices would probably fit Paul's category of "harmful words," which he would urge us to avoid.

But Paul doesn't leave us there. He accents the positive, the use of helpful words, words that are "useful for building up, as there is need, so that your words may give grace to those who hear" (Eph. 4:29). The Good News translation puts it this way: "Use helpful words, the kind that build up and provide what is needed, so that what you say will do good to those who hear you."[4] I think of one of the most highly valued members of a board on which I serve. This person asks more questions than any other member, but his questions almost always have the effect of being helpful and so his colleagues are "built up" rather than "torn down."

A final word from the Pauline tradition is to be gracious. Paul says, "Be angry but do not sin; do not let the sun go down on your anger . . . and be kind to one another, tenderhearted, forgiving one another, as God in Christ has forgiven you" (Eph. 4: 26, 32). We can't underestimate the importance of grace and forgiveness in the life of the community. Paul understood that he could not and did not live up to his own counsel; he needed the grace of God and the grace of others. And so do we all. We need grace to ask and to be asked for forgiveness, grace to forgive and grace to be forgiven. We need to let go of guilt and blame so we can forgive one another. And we need occasions of laughter and joy, of worship and praise, for these are occasions that nurture the common good and celebrate the common life.

You may say that there is plenty of good theory in what I have observed about the Christian tradition and political life, but does it work? Does it make a difference for the Christian in the public square? In view of what I said at the outset about human nature and Niebuhr's words concerning political life—it works imperfectly. And that is why grace is so essential to our life in the political arena. Poll after poll tells us that citizens are generally turned off by negative campaign tactics, by "harmful words." They would rather have campaigns be positive. There is evidence that this theory works in practice. In the election just concluded we can point to campaigns that were conducted well, where the focus was on issues and the candidates obviously respected one another. Both citizens and candidates were well served. I think of the end of the presidential campaign when candidates Dole and Clinton came to agreement about the need for campaign reform and exhibited their innate and consistent respect for each other. I also recall the President's election night awareness of the need to come together as a nation, to work across partisan lines on behalf of the common good. Indeed, across the social spectrum there is more talk and action of the collaborative sort in areas as diverse as health care, education, industry, and politics. And on Friday evening's "Late Night with David Letterman"

Bob Dole's humor and informality was grace for him and for the whole public square.

We have examples even closer at hand, right here on our campus. This past spring we discovered that the tenure policy of the college, which was shaped by faculty and administrative officers more than a decade ago, was leading to some unexpected problems. In the months that followed, we aired out this issue, and the dialogue continues today. I am confident that out of the political tradition that characterizes this academic community together we will find a just and workable solution. And lately we have been in conversation about whether or not the college should consider breaking ground with new academic programs. Again we have been airing out that question and have lately resolved to pursue all of the underlying issues and ramifications in a thoughtful, deliberative process. Again, I am confident that our political tradition will serve us well in this matter.

Across this campus there are those common but essential graces that build community and affirm the neighbor: the grace of noon basketball and a noon walk, the grace of coffee and conversation at a common table, the grace of high fives among teammates after an errant play, the grace of good-natured kidding and guffaw laughter at the end of a tense conversation, the grace of pulling together amidst issues that separate us, and the grace of surprising acts of affirmation and recognition. When the Christian moves into the public square on campus or in the church council, on the hall council or in the legislature, there is good advice and insight in our tradition. And best of all, there is grace upon which we can, and inevitably must, lean. So may we claim Paul's hope as our own, "Keep on doing the things that you have learned and received and heard and seen in me, and the God of peace will be with you" (Phil. 4:9).

Amen

Faith and Suffering

Isaiah 40:6-8

We lately have passed through the changing of the seasons. After a spectacular fall with many colored flowers and persistently green grass and full-leafed trees, the cool breezes came and finally the act of nature that we call the killing frost. Following that, in brief days, the leaves fell by the basket full, the flowers gave up their color, the grass became gray, and we observed the death of summer. It was the occasion for a certain kind of sorrow.

What happened in nature underscores the reality of death and suffering in the lives of human beings. Ten days ago as deer hunting season began, two innocent bystanders, one in her home and the other in his car, were seriously hurt by stray bullets. Two days ago, my college classmate and colleague faculty member Orland Rourke was stricken by a heart attack and died. Nearly every day a marriage that seemed good turns shaky and is then dissolved—often leaving victims. In Mogadishu, Somalia, alumna Dr. Susan Vitalis told of an orphan boy whose parents had both been killed in the war. He came, malnourished, to live in a refugee camp. But he did not seem to get better even though he was being given milk powder and high protein biscuits every time the medical team came to his camp. Then the team members learned that the camp leaders were taking his food and giving it to healthier children. They gave the orphan just enough food to keep him alive so that the relief workers would continue to bring food for him. They calculated that they were keeping many children alive by sacrificing this one.

It seems ironic that at the dawn of this season of nature's death we begin to anticipate the season of Thanksgiving. But lest we miss or trivialize the gifts for which we will soon give thanks, let us pause to reflect on the persistent, unfinished reality of human suffering. What shall we make of suffering? Where does it fit in the Christian story?

According to the distinguished theologian Douglas John Hall, there are two classic responses to suffering. At one extreme there is cynicism and at the other credulity.[1] For the cynic, suffering is the inevitable and only reality. Job flirted with this cynicism, and the prophet voiced it in the words from our text, "All people are grass, their constancy is like the flower of the field" (Isa. 40:6). For the cynic there is only tragedy, death, and sorrow—sooner or later it is inevitable. There's no room in this view for joy or pleasure, no room for hope of the transcendent. For the credulous, on the other hand, suffering is a myth or merely an obstacle to be overcome. Think positive thoughts, consume the magic potion, exercise twenty minutes three days a week, use the right deodorant and all will be well. Suffering and sorrow will be overcome.

The challenge, and the possibility, for the person of faith is to live between cynicism and credulity in the knowledge that while suffering is real, it is not the final reality for God. The God of the cross is in fact preoccupied with suffering and committed to overcoming it in the last day. The flower fades but the Word endures.

Homily over? Not quite, for the issues are complex and the tension between cynicism and credulity is real. So stay a little longer—not for the answer, but at the least for a perspective, one gleaned principally from my recent summer study in the work of Douglas John Hall. To begin, let us affirm the reality of suffering: yes, children are abused; yes, poor children do not have a fair chance at nearly anything; yes, marriages do fail and people are hurt; yes, people of color and homosexuals face discrimination; yes, disease and accidental trauma work their way through individual lives without respect for time or place, class or color, creed or connection; yes, suffering is real, excruciating, inevitable, arbitrary.

But consider this "stand alongside" proposition: some forms of suffering belong to the created order. They are a part of humans being human. Douglas John Hall provides these four examples: Loneliness is a form of sorrow. Sometimes being alone is good, it is something you have sought, but oftentimes being alone means feeling incomplete, disconnected, and even disconsolate. In the creation story, Adam came to experience loneliness. But without that experience he would not have known the ecstasy of his partnership with Eve, so what began as sorrow turned to joy. Thus loneliness served the creative order of life.

Limits are a second reality of life. We are all conscious of our respective personal limitations—limited power, limited intelligence, limited perspective. And we are also conscious of the limits in our environment—limited resources, limits beyond which we will experience harm. But as we become conscious of limits, both personal and contextual, we also become open to the possibilities of wonder, surprise, and gratitude. Indeed, sometimes we can transcend our limits, or find joy in spite of or within those limits.

Temptation is another reality. In the Eden narrative humankind became conscious of the idea that it might exceed the limits of its creaturehood. It was tempted to do so, and in yielding to that temptation experienced an avalanche of pain and suffering. The same is true for us when we give in to such temptation. But lacking the knowledge of temptation, how are we be able to judge between righteousness and evil, between truth and falsehood, between virtue and dishonor, between faithfulness and disobedience, between sin and goodness? When temptation is ignored—when anything goes—life loses its grandeur and the human spirit drowns in apathy or sensuousness.

Anxiety is the fourth form of suffering that has a creative purpose. Yes, anxiety may lead to despair. But could we, in the absence of anxiety, ever know joy, relief, and exuberance?

While Hall holds up these forms of suffering as life-giving and creative, he is emphatic in distinguishing forms of suffering that destroy life, including the proverbial idea that suffering is somehow good for you. When the creation groans in travail because of our neglect and abuse, there is nothing redeeming about the suffering. When children die from malnutrition induced by a tyrant for political ends, there is nothing creative about that suffering. When the unborn are aborted for convenience, there are only tears in paradise. When wives in a second world nation are stoned for their barrenness, there is no good thing in their suffering. When a Christian experiences such suffering, they may cry out with Job: "Today also my complaint is bitter" (Job 23:2). Or with the psalmist they may ask, "How long, O Lord? Will you forget me forever? . . . How long must I bear pain in my soul ? . . . How long shall my enemy be exalted over me?" (Ps. 13:1-2).

Professor Hall's distinctions and categories are helpful as we seek to find a place for suffering in our understanding of life and faith. But in the final analysis suffering is not a category or an abstraction, it is an experience, a reality that we can only see "in a mirror, dimly" (1 Cor. 13:12). God hears the cries; it is why God's only Son became a suffering servant, our suffering servant. It is why God's servants have been called to resist evil, to do good, to care for those who suffer. In the words of Paul: "[God] consoles us in all our affliction, so that we may be able to console those who are in any affliction with the consolation with which we ourselves are consoled by God" (2 Cor. 1:4).

We do well and wise on this eve of Thanksgiving to not only recount our blessings but also to take account of our suffering and the suffering around us—the suffering that is life-giving for which we may give thanks, the suffering that is life destroying for which we collectively pray for forgiveness, and the suffering that we do not understand for which we pray for grace and forbearance. And it is the season to pray that God, who promises to be with us, will grant us the grace, the power, and the discernment to engage the powers of evil in the world.

Let us pray with confidence to God who has the final word. "The grass withers, the flower fades; but the word of our God will stand forever" (Isa. 40:8).

Amen

Faith and Unity

1 Corinthians 12:1-12

A familiar Shaker song assures us:

> *'Tis the gift to be simple, 'tis the gift to be free*
> *'Tis the gift to come down where we ought to be*
> *And when we find ourselves in the place just right*
> *'Twill be in the valley of love and delight.*[1]

But the matter of employing gifts in a community is not always a simple thing. Paul acknowledged as much when he wrote, "Now concerning spiritual gifts, brothers and sisters, I do not want you to be misinformed" (1 Cor. 12:1). It is clear in the text that, in Paul's judgment, some were misinformed. He went on to discuss the ways in which both unity and variety are essential to faithful communities. Paul's words seem worthy of reflection during these new year's days on a small patch of acres where we are trying to understand and reconcile both our unity and our variety.

To begin where Paul does, where does our unity lie in this community we call Concordia College? Some would say, most often with sarcasm, that the unity of Concordia lies in its Norwegian ethnic heritage. We should not dismiss the importance of our Norwegian heritage. One has only to consider the place of the arts, the religious tradition, our global impulse, and the informal ethos of our common life to realize the considerable and continuing impact of that heritage. But that is not the essence of our unity as a community of learners. No, we are more diverse than that, reflecting both the changing ethnic landscape of our nation and region and the global claims of our Norwegian founders.

Another proposition is that the essence of our unity is to be found in our Lutheran identity. To be sure, one cannot fully understand this place without taking our denominational identity into account. It has rich theological and cultural meaning. In this new age of perspectival knowledge, religious and denominational particularity are being acknowledged as assets and scholars of higher education are offering encouragement to denominationally self-conscious institutions that help to create and preserve the rich mosaic of American higher education. And the quality of ecumenical and interfaith conversations, of growing importance in this country, depends upon partners who can draw upon their respective traditions in a competent way.

But our denominational identity does not define the essence of our unity as a college. For one thing, Lutherans don't all look and sound alike; one doesn't have to be around them long to recognize that. Indeed, we sometimes wear our theological, doctrinal, and liturgical diversity as a badge of family identity. And for another thing, Lutherans have a tradition of theological openness that stands at the polar opposite of a dogmatically confessing community in which people are expected to hold uniform beliefs and practice a narrow and conforming lifestyle. For example, one would search in vain for a Lutheran "party line" about academic life or academic community. And again, this Lutheran place with Norwegian roots sees itself making ecumenical claims to an increasing global audience. While we don't always do that effectively, we do understand that mandate.

So if the essence of our unity is not defined by ethnic or denominational identity—and one could add geographical and national to the list—then wherein lies our identity? The first lesson from this text is that our unity is in Christ: "Now there are varieties of gifts, but the same Spirit; and there are varieties of services, but the same Lord; and there are varieties of activities; but it is the same God who activates all of them in everyone" (1 Cor. 12:4).

Who is this spirit, this Lord, this God? The Christ who came to us in Bethlehem, whose blessing came to a diverse lot of people—rich and poor, righteous and sinners, Jews and Gentiles. And the blessing is that the many would become one. Very different—even people often in contention with one another—would find their unity in Christ. This was and is a gift and it was and is free!

The second lesson from this text concerning our unity has to do with the use of our particular gifts. "To each," said Paul "is given the manifestation of the Spirit for the common good" (1 Cor. 12:7). Amidst the variety of our gifts, unity is found in Christ and in the use of our various gifts for the common good; that is, for the good of the community. If the basis of our unity is as children of God rather than children of Knute, or of Luther or Calvin or St. Thomas, or of Asia or Africa or Latin America or Europe (blessed as these families are one and all)—if the basis of our unity is as children of God, then imagine the strength in that. And if the purpose of that unity is not primarily the glorification of our own tribe or nation or creed but the common good, well imagine the possibilities. We may in fact make music with the herald angels.

The possibilities for the common good in this community are enormous, and I may add with pleasure, demonstrable. Let me focus on the key dimension of our common life: the calling of this community is learning, learning in the service of both our present and future discipleship. To that common calling we bring variety—a variety of styles and tasks, a variety of talents and temperaments, a variety of disciplines and pedagogies. And the common good around which we rally these diverse gifts is learning.

We are called upon in these days to apply with diligence our diverse gifts. The center of our agenda is not goodtime weekends, though we do want you to have good times on the weekends. Nor is the center of our agenda championship athletic teams, though if we are talented and disciplined we will enjoy our share of glory. No, the center of the agenda at this place is learning—free, disciplined, and hopefully delightful learning—but, if not, so be it. And the goal of learning is excellence, not institutional glory but your personal best, whatever that may be. All of us—teachers, students and administrative staff—have responsibility for that common goal. I think that basically we have that straight. We have a hardworking faculty and staff with high expectations for themselves and each other and a deep mutual respect. And you students, both in and out of the classroom, reflect diligence and commitment to excellence.

There are times and circumstances in which we fail to apply our gifts with diligence. Last semester some students did not succeed at that task. In some very few cases it was a matter of a mismatch between the gifts of the individual and the expectations of the college, and the earlier such discoveries are made, the better. But most who did not succeed last semester could have and should have. There were failures of self-discipline in some cases, failures of inspiration in others, failures in tough love and discipline in still others. A number of students were not permitted to return to the college this term for academic reasons. Our analysis indicates that twenty-five percent of those students did not seek out the gifts of our academic support services. Another twenty-five percent of those students were not referred to our helping services by any of their teachers. These stark facts reveal that we still have a ways to go in stewarding the gifts of this community for the common good. Individually and collectively we are challenged to be conscientious in cultivating our individual gifts of teaching, learning, and caring.

Our unity is based on a common gift and a common calling. The gift is the unity that is ours as a family of believers. And our calling is to use our diverse gifts for the common good. So we begin this new semester with high resolve and with the common goal of glorifying the God who is the source of our unity, the author of our gifts and the voice of our calling.

Amen

Faith and Wealth

Mark 10:17-27

A quick read of this text from Mark may tell us that it is the story of a wealthy man who has a bad day with Jesus. And the moral of the story is that wealth may be hazardous to the health of your soul. It is, most of us may assume, a story about someone else because our employer or our banker or our credit card company knows that we are not wealthy. But if we stay with this text a little while and probe its truth, we just may find ourselves in the story.

Let's begin with the man in the story and see what else the text tells us about him in addition to the fact that he was wealthy. In the first place it tells us that this man sought after truth and righteousness. Jesus asked him if he kept the commandments, particularly those dealing with the neighbor. Yes, he said, I have done so from my youth. And we might surmise—since he was a keeper of the law, one who wanted to do the right thing—that he was a tither, giving ten percent of his wealth to the poor and to the widows and orphans. A very good man!

We also know from this text that he was restless. In spite of doing good, things were not right in his life. Consider the first verse of the text, "A man ran up and knelt before [Jesus], and asked him, 'Good Teacher, what must I do to inherit eternal life?'" (Mark 10:17). In spite of his good deeds and acts of righteousness, actions that Jesus affirmed, the man's life was unsettled. The late Lutheran scholar Joseph Sittler observed the disquiet of the spirit and mind, and saw what he believed to be signs of the formation of the human soul. Something stood between this man and the freedom of his soul to live with God and he knew it. He didn't know what it was but Jesus did—it was money. We know from the witness of the gospel that Jesus taught people with a variety of things standing between them and God. For some it was the law, for others power, for others knowledge, for others self-centeredness, and for still others it was poverty, leprosy, demons, and sins of the flesh.

Now we may find ourselves in this text. We all thirst for God. We may be trying our self-disciplined, level best consistently to do the right thing—keeping the moral laws, tithing, and doing acts of charity. But at the same time we may be experiencing a kind of restlessness, a nagging crisis of bondage. As St. Augustine confessed to God, "Thou hast formed us for Thyself, and our hearts are restless till they find rest in Thee."[1]

But, you say, this text is about a particular kind of bondage, about the bondage of wealth. So, you say, that leaves me out. I will wait for next week's text. Well maybe so and maybe not. In the first place, money as an all-consuming obsession can as easily separate a relatively poor person from God as it can a rich one. But more to the point, in a world of relative wealth, we are among the wealthiest. We in America constitute about one fifth of the world's population but control four fifths of the world's wealth. Yes, even with our mortgages and credit card debt we are among the very rich. Note that the disciples were of modest means financially. When Jesus turned to them after speaking to the rich man we are told that even they were astonished at his radical counsel, for they realized that it applied to them as well. So if by this time you think that you may in fact be in the text, consider what Jesus has to say to us.

First, it is clear that wealth can be hazardous to our souls. If you are hooked on money it will be harder for you to get to heaven, that is, to be with God, than it will be for a camel to pass through the eye of a needle. (That figure of speech reveals both the clarity and humor of Christ.) If money runs your life, whether you are living on ten dollars a day or ten thousand dollars an hour, your soul is not free to live with God.

Tough love is a tired cliché, but if ever it fit, it fits here. Jesus came down hard on this man. He said that if money was keeping him from God, he was better off without it. Sell everything, Jesus advised. This is not consistent with a therapeutic model that would explain away the obsession and perhaps bless it and prolong it. No, it is more like the Twelve Step model that says if alcohol is your obsession, or gambling, or duplicity, or fantasy violence—then stop it altogether. Everything else in our lives may seem to be going all right, but if this one thing is destroying our relationship with God and neighbor, then we need to deal with it. Jesus didn't disguise the cross; he placed it in the foreground under the spotlight. And when the disciples asked, "Do you mean us too?" he said yes, I mean you too.

And what was tough about what Jesus said was also full of love. Early in the story, after the man gave an account of his remarkable stewardship, we are told, "Jesus, looking at him loved him" (Mark 10:21). He saw the man's possibilities; he perceived the man's needs and spoke the truth to him. And the love with which he spoke and acted was love that was and is capable of transforming life, both present and future. And Jesus told the disciples in their confusion over all of this, "For God all things are possible" (Mark 10:27).

And so it is. Paul spoke about the renewal of our minds, which occurs when God breaks down the barriers that separate us from God. Jesus saw the possibilities in stiff-necked Peter, in James and John who longed for status, in Martha who wanted things done right, and in the Samaritan woman with a clouded past. Jesus is prepared to do for us what he did for all of them. And Jesus knows better than we understand the restlessness of our souls. He is prepared to speak to us in tough words of truth. He is prepared to transform our lives by the renewal of our spirits. Jesus is prepared to stand by us in valleys full of shadow. Jesus is prepared to do the impossible and the improbable.

So come, Lord Jesus, be our guest.

Amen

Faith and Work

Matthew 21:33-43

In my early years our family lived on a rented farm in western Minnesota. The landlord lived in a town nearby where he ran the stockyards. His name was Bill Tillman. He was a Catholic, we were Lutherans, and so ecumenism had an early start in our neighborhood. Bill was a good person and an excellent landlord. He built a new house and granary on our farm. He took an interest in our family. In the summer he often came to look at the crops and visit with my dad under the big cottonwood tree. Bill never had to ask my dad for his share of the crop; for my dad that was automatic. Bill trusted and respected my father and my father trusted and respected Bill.

With that background, you can perhaps understand the difficulty I had as a young person identifying with the parable of the gospel today, a parable in which the landowner was more than generous to the tenant but the tenant, ungrateful and willful, betrayed the trust. I moved through some years of Sunday school before I came to understand that the parable was an allegory and that there were layers of meaning. God is the landowner, the generous provider; the servants he sends to collect rent are the prophets; and the heir who is finally sent is God's Son, Jesus Christ. So this text is, after all, about faith in the workplace.

I could probably apply that text to the relationship between Bill Tillman and my dad. But the point of this proclamation is for today and for this vineyard, so let me invite you to consider what words of truth this story may bring to us, the tenants in this Concordia workplace. The first word that comes to mind in this text is providence.

God provided the tenants with a workplace, a vineyard, in which the grapes were already planted, the wine press was already in place, and the fences and the watchtower had already been built to make everything secure. In short, the tenants were provided for generously. Moving from the workplace of the text to the workplace of our campus, it is the case that we too have been given generous provision. One thinks of the intellectual gifts; in cross section you students rank in the upper quartile of college students in the country. And the various national rating services tell us that this is a place of quality. The achievements of faculty, staff, and students bear out this assessment. And our campus, facilities, and equipment—while always leaving something to be desired—make this a very good and complete place to carry out our callings. In addition, there are people outside of the college who are generous to this community with their gifts and affirmations of many kinds. And there are people here who care for us and for each other—teachers, friends, counselors. Indeed, people don't usually come—and surely don't stay—if they do not identify with the caring ethos of this college. All of these and more are God's good gifts to us, generous resources with which to pursue our vocations in this vineyard. Our landlord, God, is indeed generous.

A second word in this text is freedom. The tenants were given the run of their workplace, the vineyard. The landlord did not even send an overseer, a farm manager if you will, to keep track of things. Indeed, we are told that he went to another country. In this Concordia vineyard we also have freedom. During the welcoming week each year I tell both new students and their families that they will find uncommon freedom here. Students, you choose your friends without the oversight of family, you decide on your courses and how much or how little you will study. You decide how busy you will be, whether or not you will go to class, get your assignments in on time, and all the rest. And you make key decisions about how you will care for mind and body and spirit. During that first week we talk about the freedom of mind and body and spirit. You find all kinds of ideas and options here and plenty of lessons, precepts and examples—but ultimately, you are going to choose for yourself what you will believe and how you will think. That freedom of conscience is axiomatic.

A third word in this text is accountability. That is really the pervasive word in this text. It is a word we might prefer to avoid. Indeed, this is a text we might rather dodge. Theologian Soren Kierkegaard described the tendency of the age toward texts like this in this way:

"The method now is to leave out the existentially strenuous passages in the New Testament. We hush them up—and then we arrange things on easier and cheaper terms. We probably think that since we did not mention these passages God does not know that they are in the New Testament."[1]

But this text is before us today straight and unavoidable. And it tells us that while the tenants were free to run the farm, they were finally accountable by the landlord who ultimately sent people to collect his share of the crop. We would understand from this text that in this well-provisioned workplace we call Concordia—a place to grow and change and prosper—we are ultimately accountable. We are accountable for the gifts God provides to us here. We are accountable through those agents whom God calls to serve here— the faculty and staff. We are accountable to our circle of family and advocates. And ultimately, we are accountable to God who placed us in this vineyard.

These are the days of midterm exams, which gives this notion of accountability special meaning. For first-year students it is an especially important time, hopefully a good time to test your habits and review your priorities and progress. But it is not just students who are accountable in this vineyard; we all are—teachers for their teaching, pastors for their proclamation, caregivers for their ministries, and managers for their stewardship.

Beyond our specific callings, we are accountable in a large sense as well to the mission that connects this college and each of us with the larger community. I shall not attempt to review all of the elements of that call, but it does suggest clearly our accountability to service, to responsible conduct, to the life of the spirit and the life of the mind, to life in community. When the citizens of communities like ours neglect their call, the consequences are serious. In a world full of other calls—calls to violence, to special interest, to self, to materialism, to fear—we would do well to remember what God has called us to be and to do in this place.

A fourth word I wish to lift up from this text is mercy. The master in the parable provided the vineyard, entrusted it to his tenants and kept coming back to them. One servant was stoned, another killed, another beaten—but the master kept on sending them. Finally he sent his Son. This God of our vineyard does not deal with us according to our stewardship but according to his love. We stoned the prophets, but others were sent. We crucified Jesus the Christ, but God sent the Holy Spirit to dwell with us. And so it is in our workplace. Sometimes we are simply unable to measure up to our calling here and we will grieve for that. Other times, by intention, we may betray the trust that the landlord has placed upon us in this place. But God, who is the landlord of this vineyard and each of us, is persistent in mercy. Christ makes intercession for us and the Holy Spirit dwells in our midst even now. And that is why the final word in this text, which emphasizes accountability, is a gospel word, the word of mercy.

James Ford, a Lutheran pastor who served for two decades as chaplain of the United States House of Representatives observed a great deal of power—political, military, economic, intellectual—during his years of public service. But he maintained that the power of grace—a power of an entirely different kind—surpassed all others. Nothing else even comes close. Grace is a free gift that releases us from our isolation and bondage, from pain and guilt, from the worst that can possibly come our way.

To all of the tenants in this our vineyard, God has sent these words: a word of providence, a word of freedom, a word of accountability and a word of grace—persistent and enduring. Take these words—all of them—with you into this week of your life in this vineyard of the Lord.

Amen

PART TWO

Seasons of Faith

For Everything There Is a Season

This collection includes homilies I preached on particular occasions in the academic year or various junctures in the church year. These two "years" traverse the same time, though not the same chronology. Each in its own way divides into seasons, offering yet another measure of the passage of time. But seasons are not merely markers on the calendar. They shape and reflect the pulse of life, offering opportunities time and again throughout the year to address key questions of faith: Who are we as Christians? What are we called to be and to do in the world?

Every year has a beginning. The opening convocation convening a new academic year presents students and faculty with an opportunity to reflect on the nature of the academic enterprise and our mission in the world. Advent, which ushers in a new church year, is a time to reflect on the promise of a Savior, the promise that brought colleges like Concordia into being.

Every year has an ending. The closing homily of the academic year, preached at an event we called "The Mass of Exodus," is an opportunity to think about embodying Christ's mission in the world even as friends separate from one another to go their own ways. So too, the season of Pentecost, which closes out the church year, invites people of faith to reflect on our ongoing discipleship in the world.

Most of life, however, is lived between beginnings and endings, in stretches of time given over to pursuit of knowledge, to growth in self-awareness, to increase in faith. This "between-time" is the focus of the homilies for Homecoming, for a new semester, and for the liturgical seasons of Epiphany, Lent, and Easter that fill out this collection called "The Seasons of Faith."

A Holy Restlessness

Exodus 32:24

Welcome, students. Welcome, incoming freshmen and those who have joined us from other colleges, universities, and nations of the world. Welcome also to all who return to continue your academic journey at Concordia. For those new to this campus, you have experienced some busy days filled with both the expected—registration and try-outs and meetings—and the unexpected—trips to the mall, to the parks, and to the homes of members of the faculty and staff.

You have all come to us with significant expectations. Based on data we collect from perspective Concordia students, we know that you have chosen this college because you expect to find friendly and helpful people here in the faculty and staff and among the students— and I hope that you already have. Our research tells us that another of the major reasons why you have chosen Concordia is because of the quality of the academic program and the faculty.

Many of you tell us that you have also come expecting to find a community that is serious about matters of ethics, faith, and spirituality. Indeed, social science research tells us that your generation is more serious about such matters than the generations preceding yours. You will find opportunities to explore these issues and express your faith here, for the assumption we make is that matters of faith and belief and spirituality are at the very core of human existence.

According to our research, these expectations are among the most prominent that you bring with you to this campus. These are expectations to which we are committed, and we look forward to mutual engagement around them. But the thesis of my remarks this morning is to suggest that you will find more than you expect on this campus, and I sincerely hope that one of those discoveries will be what I call "a holy restlessness."

Let me illustrate that "holy restlessness" with a couple of ancient, but well-known anecdotes. The first is from Plato's *The Republic*. On the way back from a festival in Athens, Socrates and his companions were discussing the question, "What is justice?" Is it helping your friends or hurting your enemies? Is it giving everyone what he or she deserves? As the conversation rolled on, folks got restless with Socrates because he would critique every person's answer to the questions he raised, but he would never venture his own opinion. At last one of those students, Thrasymachus, said something to the effect of, "Where do you get off, Socrates, teasing people into offering definitions while you offer none, and then when they volunteer an answer, you just score points off of their attempts?" Ah, the restlessness of unanswered and perhaps unanswerable questions!

The other anecdote comes from the book of Genesis, the story of Jacob and Esau. Let me retell it. Jacob had deceived his father and thus deprived his brother Esau of the inheritance that was coming to him. Many years passed and finally there was a showdown between the two brothers, each now with substantial holdings and armies. On the eve of the showdown, Jacob, racked by years of guilt and uncertainty over what he had done to his brother, lay down on the ground, and we are told in Genesis 32:24, "a man wrestled with him until daybreak." That man, it is clear, was God's messenger, for in the morning he blessed Jacob, and in the days following, Jacob and Esau would be reconciled and Jacob would become the progenitor of a great nation. For Jacob, that night had been—literally—a holy restlessness.

Now, the stakes will be different for you than they were for Thrasymacus and Jacob—but still, I wish for you too a holy restlessness. The first restlessness that you may encounter is in the relationship between your special academic interest and the liberal arts goals of this college. Many of you have an idea about a major or an eventual career and that is all right. Surely the world out there needs increasing numbers of managers, teachers, accountants, doctors, lawyers, nurses, artists, social workers, writers, therapists, and entrepreneurs of many kinds. This will incline you to focus on a major, on a career—to dig deep to cover all of the bases. But the curriculum of this college creates rather deliberately a tension here, for it requires courses far outside any specialty you may choose—courses in the sciences and arts, in religion and the humanities, and other disciplines that constitute what we call the liberal arts.

We mean, we intend, to create a restlessness between your specific interest and the core curriculum for a couple of reasons. First of all, if you plan to teach, for example, the Spanish language, you will discover that you will teach it more competently if you know something about Spanish history and Spanish art and Spanish religion and the list goes on. Or, a career in science or health science may be your goal, but in encountering vexing questions about the end of life, or cloning, or stem cells, you will need the help of ethicists and philosophers, of economists and social scientists.

There is another reason why this restlessness is constructive. In a national study, employers, the people who hire accountants and managers and investors and human service people, identified the primary skills they look for in perspective employees. Here is a sample of those skills: respect for others, an appreciation for culture, loyalty, interest, and integrity, civic values, a love for learning and problem solving skills. Such skills are at the heart of the liberal arts, and they will make of your restlessness a constructive engagement.

A second source of restlessness is one of which most of you are already aware, either by experience or observation, and that is the restlessness that comes in trying to reconcile our need for unity as a people and the reality of our diversity. We are part of a global community, characterized by diversity of race, ethnicity, language, culture, religion, and political and economic systems. We recognize diversity as a good. Think about our food: Italian pizza, French onion soup, Norwegian lefse, Mexican tortillas, Tansanian ougaley, and

Ghanan fufu or chicken beer-ah-nay from Bangladesh. Similarly, think about our art, our music, our humor, our notions of excellence and hospitality. All are enriched by the influence of diverse traditions. As Pope John Paul II said, "To cut one's self off from the reality of difference—or, worse, to attempt to stamp out that difference—is to cut oneself off from the possibility of sounding the depths of the mystery of human life".[1]

The other side of the balancing act is our need and desire for unity. For example, it is necessary that we have sufficient unity in our communities to secure our common good around such issues as education, safety, human services, and economic development. Again, in the words of Pope John Paul II, "We must *overcome our fear of the future. But we will not be able to overcome it completely unless we do so together*".[2]

There you have the case for diversity and the case for unity. They are both essential and thus desirable, and that is the source of our restlessness. In Eastern Europe, in the Middle East, in the subcontinent of Africa, and in English speaking Northern Ireland, diversity is a simmering cauldron that boils over regularly with catastrophic results.

In America, as we grow more diverse, we are tempted to grow more contentious and insecure. As novelist Anais Nin is credited with saying, "We don't see things as they are, we see things as we are."[3] A survey by the Joint Center for Political and Economic Studies a few years ago dramatized that reality. Only twenty-one percent of white Americans surveyed perceived that there is significant discrimination against black Americans, while fifty percent of black Americans saw it the other way. Indeed, "we don't see things as they are, we see things as we are." Think about your perspective on unity if you or your people are being marginalized by the decisions of duly elected, majoritarian boards or commissions. "We don't see things as they are, we see things as we are." There is indeed a restlessness as we seek to reconcile the richness and reality of diversity with our longing for, and the necessity of, unity. In this college community we hope that restlessness will move you to thoughtfulness and to responsible action.

You will find opportunities to appreciate and apprehend diversity here. In your classes you will encounter diversity in myriad forms. Urban and global study experiences will provide another opportunity to shape your perceptions, to shape who you are, and in effect, to change "who we are." Lectures, concerts, and festivals will feature the diversity of the world. In the life of this campus community, you will have opportunities to live together, to work together for our common good today and the common good of the world tomorrow. And the word is that your "millennial generation" is both equipped and inclined to build community on this campus and beyond it.

Let me describe a third source of restlessness, the restlessness we find in the tension between suffering and hope. We live in a world full of inequities. Ours is a thriving economy for which we are grateful, but in America, the wealthy are doing much better than those who are poor, the progress is very unequal. For example, in 2001, ten percent of our population lived below the poverty level as did sixteen percent of our children in this the wealthiest nation in the world. Does that make you restless?

Billions are being spent on exotic medical initiatives, including artificial hearts, kidneys, knees, and spinal disks—while at the same time, millions cannot afford minimal healthcare. To be specific, we spend sixteen percent of our gross national product on healthcare— by far the highest percentage in the developed world, but one sixth of our population is without health insurance. Does that make you restless?

While 1.2 billion people in the world live in poverty, here in the United States, we spend $7 billion dollars a year on video rentals, $20 billion on jewelry, $24 billion for alcohol, but only $4.4 billion for global development assistance. Does that make you restless?

Well let's put a face on it. A story in *Newsweek* this summer introduced Henry Kiiaka, an 18-year-old Ugandan with a high school education and a job earning $30 a month keeping books for a farmer. He sported a broad smile and a bright yellow button-down shirt. According to the *Newsweek* writer, "Despite his cheerful manner, Henry is no stranger to pain. He lost his father as a child, and his mother died of AIDS three years ago, leaving him to care for his four younger siblings. Two of his three teenage sisters still refuse to admit that the disease has touched their family, but Henry doesn't have the luxury of denial. His half-brother, 10-year-old Ronnie, is living with HIV—and as head of the household, he is the boy's only lifeline. 'Sometimes I have times alone,' Henry confides while sitting with the downcast child at the pediatric clinic at Mulago Hospital. 'One or two or three drops of tears' "[4] Does the story of Henry make you restless?

Suffering and inequity—the case is easy to make. And it should make us restless. More than that, it should leave us distraught and enraged.

But what of hope? Where is it born and how is it nurtured? Hope is shaped by empathy, by our awareness of the inequities, by our sorrow for the victims, and by our desire to be of help. And hope is informed by knowledge, which is what this place is about. We know that misguided, misdirected mercy and ineffective responses may be destructive, so if informed action is essential, then academic excellence and our work on this campus is prerequisite. But we need more than knowledge. We also need the conviction of faith, faith in a God who stands with the oppressed, who heals the sick and feeds the hungry, and who calls us to reach out to our neighbor. In the words of theologian William Barclay, "The Christian hope has seen everything and endured everything, and still has not despaired, because it believes in God."[5]

That conviction is what makes our restlessness "holy." That conviction is the source of our hope, and that conviction leads us to action, to using our knowledge in the construction of helpful response. The distinguished writer and educator Sharon Daloz Parks has suggested that the restlessness we experience must be enlarged and sustained in a community of discipline, imagination, and trust.[6]

Concordia is such a community, where your restlessness will be both respected and expanded, where both secular and sacred truth are taken seriously, and where faculty care about you and the vocation you are constructing. While your primary agenda in these years is knowledge, it is not your exclusive agenda. You will find extensive opportunities to act out your hope in this community, where there are homeless people in need of food and hospitality, where there are children in need of friendship and recognition, and where there are elderly in need of comfort and company. There will be many opportunities for your hope to take on the flesh and blood of good and helpful deeds for the neighbor, and thus the restlessness of suffering leads to the embodiment of hope.

I am confident that you will find what you expect in these Concordia years—good people, excellent teaching, and quality education. And I hope that you will also find the holy restlessness of which I have spoken today. What makes it holy? It is made holy in part because of the vision of this college, which calls and prepares you to serve God and the world. And it is also made holy by God who calls us to deal with the restlessness we find in the world and in ourselves.

Jacob wrestled with uncertainty about his future. He wrestled with his anxieties, and in the course of it, he wrestled with God. When he awoke, he was blessed and moved on to do God's work. May you be blessed with such a restlessness, with such a calling, and with such fulfillment in your life.

Amen

Not So Wild a Dream

Ezekiel 37:1-14; Acts 2:1-21; John 7:37-39a

It has been a weekend of talking about memories and about dreams.
Let me tell you about a boyhood dream of mine. Our farm was just
a quarter of a mile from a meandering creek. It went by the inglori-
ous name of Mud Creek, which, sadly, was descriptive enough. In
spring and early summer it would yield fresh fish—bullheads and
bluegills—good game and good eating. And as I sat along the shore,
I often had a dreamed of building a raft and floating down Mud
Creek until it joined the Yellow Medicine River and then the Minnesota River and then, at Minneapolis, the mighty Mississippi. But,
like so many youthful dreams, my dream didn't materialize.

Years later I learned about a dream of a similar kind. Eric Sevareid, the late respected broadcast journalist and grandson of Concordia founder J.O. Haugen, grew up in Velva, North Dakota, and in
Minneapolis. As a seventeen-year-old, he and his boyhood friend,
Walter Port, dreamed of canoeing up the Minnesota River and then
down the Red River to Lake Winnipeg and on to Hudson Bay and
the North Atlantic. They challenged their dream in a 2,200-mile trip,
which Sevareid would later describe in his midlife autobiography,
Not So Wild a Dream.

But speaking of wild dreams, we have in our Old Testament
story the dream of Ezekiel. Ezekiel was a prophet in the sixth century
before Christ. By the time he had the dream described in our text
he had been a prophet for perhaps twenty years. Ezekiel's dream was
initially more like a nightmare, for he found himself set down in the
middle of a valley—a valley full of bones and, we are told, they were

very dry bones. They were the dry bones of the failed dreams and hopes for Israel, which was to have been a land flowing with milk and honey where Yahweh would be worshiped in truth and purity and where the people would respect one another within the tradition of law come down from God. But the promised kingdom was now a divided kingdom. The likes of Manasseh and Nebuchadnezzar divided the nation. The chosen people were scattered. Idolatry flourished. The astral deities from Assyria were made respectable; Manasseh had his own son pass through the fires of human sacrifice; the local sanctuaries—the holy places—became places of debauchery; and any prophet who lifted a voice was snuffed out. And so Ezekiel's dream of his nation was a dream of life in a valley full of dried bones, the very dead bones of what had once been a thriving, faithful people—and it was not so wild a dream.

Fast forward now to the first century and a Jerusalem gathering of ragtag people who were followers of Christ. Jesus had given them a commission but they wondered how he could possibly have been serious about it, for they were a people of dry bones. Jesus had talked and taught about faith, about priorities and responsibility. The disciples had heard it and seen it, but still they had great difficulty believing it and living it. They had been disloyal to Jesus in his final hours, just plain heading out to look for a place to hide, to save their own skin. Peter's betrayal was fresh in mind; Judas couldn't resist the temptation to take the money and run; James and John were still looking for status, not sacrifice; Matthew was dogged by his reputation as a tax collector; and Thomas was always, always asking questions and not quite willing to yield his total allegiance. Dry bones, very dry bones laid out in the sun for all to see.

Then there was the preposterous task to which they were supposedly called—to take the gospel into a world where people spoke many different languages and followed separate cultural traditions; a world in which the Romans kept peace by the sword; a world of religious pluralism in which Christianity was highly suspect; a world that included Athens where reason was king and where God was thought to be unknown and unknowable. Yes, these were dry bones, very dry bones laid out in the sun for all to see—dry bones—not so wild a dream.

And we can see the dry bones in our valleys, too. In Bosnia ten days ago as the army regained ground from the Serbs, it came upon an unmarked grave containing the bodies of more than 500 slaughtered in the name of blood and God and soil. In our own land there are pathologies we cannot begin to understand. Two weeks ago the Pulitzer laureate, Gwendolyn Brooks, read her poetry on campus, including a poem called "Thinking of Elizabeth Steinberg" about a child, the victim of sexual molestation. This line captures the horror of it all: "Tardy tears will not return you to air."[1]

Dry bones, very dry bones.

A September news story quoted Attorney General Janet Reno describing the 165 percent increase in the murder rate among fourteen- to seventeen-year-olds. Gwendolyn Brooks told us of young men in her city who do not expect to reach adulthood. They expect to die in the street and they are already choosing their caskets and planning their funerals right down to the guest list. One expert described them as "the young and the ruthless," but perhaps more accurately they are "the young and the hopeless." Dry bones.

We live in a country with a booming economy and a growing underclass and bulging prisons. Something doesn't compute and we all know it. Dry bones.

And our political vision is that government can't replace character, resourcefulness, or responsibility. It is a truism on which we now act, and wisely so. But who and how will we care for the "least of these" when personal stewardship and volunteerism are on the decline? Dry bones.

And there are other personal stories too—the sudden summer death of a classmate in a car crash, the slow death of another to cancer, the brokenness of a lifelong relationship, and the lack of virtue in the face of temptation. Dry bones. Very dry bones—not so wild a dream.

But there is more to Ezekiel's dream, my friends. He spent much of his prophetic ministry counting the bones and castigating the culture, heaping blame on everyone in sight. But there was a second prophecy in the dream. In the valley of the dry bones, God acted; sinew covered the dry bones and skin covered the flesh. "There was a noise, a rattling, and the bones came together, bone to its bone" (Ezek. 37:7). And then God said, "I will cause breath to enter you, and you shall live" (37:5). "And the breath came into them, and they lived, and stood on their feet, a vast multitude" (37:10). In spite of idolatry and backsliding, separation and persecution, the house of Israel was not dead after all; a new day was coming—the people of God would be restored. No more dry bones for God said, "I will put my spirit within you and you shall live."

Then think about the disciples' dream. Jesus had told them they would receive the power to bring life to the dry bones of their failed vision and their failed resolve. "You shall receive power when the Holy Spirit has come upon you," they had been told (Acts 1:8). But could they have imagined what would happen? Many people of many tongues from many nations had gathered in Jerusalem, and the Holy Spirit came upon them like the rush of a mighty wind. And the people spoke simultaneously in many languages from many different lands—Parthians, Medes, Elamites, Mesopotamians, Egyptians, Cretans, Arabs and Jews—even some guests from Rome. But the miraculous part is that they all heard the same message about God's love and deeds of power. Talk about unity amidst diversity. And in the midst of this wild gathering, Peter would stand to speak about a dream—the dream of Joel:

> "In the last days it will be, God declares,
>   that I will pour out my Spirit upon all flesh,
>   and your sons and daughters shall prophesy,
>   and your young men shall see visions,
>   and your old men shall dream dreams." (Acts 2:17)

And as the events in Jerusalem that day proved, the dream of Joel, as with the dream of Ezekiel, was not so wild a dream. The promise of Christ was made real in their midst—it was resurrection day. The doubt and division, guilt and uncertainty that had dried out the bones of the disciples were shed away, and the bones came together and God's Spirit breathed life into them. And the disciples would carry out their commission—they would carry the witness to Judea and Samaria and the ends of the earth. The breath came into them, and they stood, a great multitude. It was, after all, not so wild a dream.

And today as we gather here on our field of dreams, we nurture the dream of Ezekiel. In parishes around the globe we gather around word and sacrament and the living water renews the valleys of our dry bones and the Spirit of God enters our lives. And thus we find the resources to transcend the episodes of doubt, despair, and brokenness that hound our days. And in our human communities we find the will to persist in our claim that what unifies us as children of God is far more powerful than what divides us into religious, ethnic, and political categories. When the Spirit of God enters the dry bones of our church we discover that our gospel mission transcends our divisions over polity and policy. On the global scene, Palestinian and Israeli leaders painstakingly attempt to carve a new path of peace where there had been only a trail of blood—they are surely not unaware of Ezekiel's later dreams of a just and peaceful kingdom—and we can believe that God's life-giving, peacemaking spirit is in their company. And in our neighborhoods when increasingly multicultural neighbors reach out in mutual understanding and commitment we can see the bones rising—and it is not so wild a dream.

In these days of our homecoming we have shared countless stories of people whose dreams bear the mark of God's transforming Spirit. There is the Cobber physician who brings healing to refugees in this world's most desperate places and there is another who brings hospice care to the dying. There is a Native American who now administers justice in the state court and an entrepreneur whose passion is to create jobs where people most need them. There are scores upon scores of teachers committed to excellence and nurture; there are public servants committed to both justice and prudence; and there are thousands of friends who have discovered the joy of giving life and livelihood away.

And on this campus site a new generation of Cobbers shares the dream. Students reach out to those in need across the street and down the block and around the world in such an array of caregiving that we have simply lost count. And the words "calling and vocation" are a respected and often spoken part of the daily vocabulary of staff and faculty and students alike. Is there brokenness here? Of course, and the dry bones that go with it. But the dream is alive here for the word of the Lord is alive here. And when that word and that dream are alive—so too is the breath of God.

In such places as this and in such lives as ours, God declares: "I will pour out my Spirit upon all flesh, and your sons and your daughters shall prophesy, and your young shall see visions, and your old shall dream dreams."

And that is not so wild a dream!

Amen

Salty Days and Starry Nights

1 Peter 2:9-17; Matthew 5:13-16

Salty days and starry nights. In harvest season our farm was a lively place. There were always extra hired men to haul bundles and hired girls to help with the food. Young boys like me were confined to the grain wagons—safely out of harm's way and with our own chore of keeping the load leveled. And during the day there was always a crossing breeze at the threshing site and the chaff would fill our shoes and cuffs and collars.

The August sun burned especially bright in harvest season, reaching into the 90s on what seemed then to be frequent occasions. It was hot and hard and dirty work the livelong day. And to maintain good health one needed to sweat—if that body system failed, folks fainted dead away in what we called heat prostration. Since an ounce of prevention was worth a pound of cure, there were always salt tablets by the water jug. And at day's end shirt collars and scoop shovel and pitchfork handles carried the gray residue of salt that had done its job of cleansing the body and sustaining the strength—strength needed to do hard work.

When we finished a field or wound up the harvest we would often gather at sundown around the back step by the big box elder tree. Dad would bring home from town an ice-cold watermelon and we would have a celebration. And as the celebration wound down we lay on the grass and looked at the stars—calling out the constellations and venturing our dreams. Those starry nights of celebration were a time of joy, of thanks, of anticipation. Such were the salty days and starry nights in the harvest times of my childhood.

Each of us needs salt and light in the harvest times of our lives. For many there is a harvest of want. Our economy booms, but according to political scientist Andrew Hacker, the percentage of U.S. citizens in prison or on the streets outpaces any other advanced nation, as does the number of neglected children.

There is the harvest of separation. We are an increasingly diverse nation in which the walls of separation grow higher, accompanied by meanness of spirit. As President Clinton pointed out at the recent commemoration of the integration of the Little Rock schools, "Segregation is no longer the law, but too often segregation is still the rule."[1]

And we also experience the harvest of moral ambiguity. Indeed, the lines have become blurred even among the best and the brightest. In a survey of young people named to "Who's Who Among American High School Students," seventy percent acknowledged that they had cheated in school and most said it was "no big deal." According to a national survey by the American Board of Family Practice, the young are not "happy campers"—three of four teenagers believe the world their parents lived in was better than the one in which they live; half believe the world their children inherit will be worse than the world in which they are living; three of four believe environmental pollution will affect the health of everyone; six of ten expect someone in their family to be a victim of crime; and six of ten expect that someone in their family will get AIDS.

In this age of highly tuned technology we have extended life and made living more comfortable to the point of forgetting the tragic and the unpredictable. Then there is the irony of the spacecraft Mir's disenabling, the unpredictability of human relationships, and the unplanned reality of cancer. It reminds one of the age-old question, "Do you know how to make God laugh? Tell him your plans." Such is the harvest of the lives we live out one by one. There is sweat in our harvest time, darkness in its nights—we need salt and we need light.

We need salt and light in the harvest times of our communities, too. Michael J. Sandel, a professor of government at Harvard

University, in writing about "democracy's discontent," observed that despite our affluence our common life is beset by anxiety and frustration. We are, increasingly, surrounded by bureaucracies that require us to fill out forms and be in compliance; by care providers who seem driven more by the hard-edged economics of a distant insurance company than the reality of our needs; by service providers who bombard us with promises and then serve us with conditions; by churches that are strong on symbols but weak on connections; by schools that are expected to do more than is reasonable with less than is necessary; by political representatives who may be compromised by deep pockets and a public discourse which is increasingly discordant. As Sandel sees it, there are two sources of discontent, one is fear that "we are losing control of the forces that govern our lives," and the other is the sense that "the moral fabric of community is unraveling around us."[2] Whatever your take on the state of community in America there is sweat in our harvest time and darkness in our nights—we need salt and we need light.

And it's harvest time for the church. In the faith community we are a church living with the challenges of religious pluralism—we are no longer the only game in town. And beyond the faith community we are a church living in a post-Christian era facing the challenge of connecting with a society that increasingly regards us as harmless, powerless, or irrelevant. Thus we face the twin temptations of becoming remnant communities on the one hand or, on the other, clones of the secular society, offering help but not holiness.

And we are a church facing a harvest of ignorance. George Gallup in a survey of young people found that only thirty-five percent could name all four Gospels; forty-four percent did not know how many disciples Jesus had; and twenty-nine percent did not know the religious event associated with Easter. It's harvest time—there are estimated to be 120 million non-Christians in this land. Perhaps that is why churches in Africa—churches that are growing by leaps and bounds—are sending thousands of missionaries abroad including to the United States. Yes, it's harvest season for the church and we are in need of salt and light.

And it's harvest time in the colleges and universities of our land. By the midpoint of this century rationalism had marginalized religious study at most colleges and universities in our country, including many of those established by the church. The intellectual credo of the '60s and '70s was that if you couldn't weigh or measure or quantify a thing, it was nonsense. And the goal of enlightenment theology was to free ourselves from dogma and tradition by practicing the virtues of "skepticism, tolerance, and individual freedom." All of which lead author Anthony B. Robinson to conclude that the modern academic project was "far more successful in dismantling the tradition than in rebuilding or sustaining lives and communities of faith."[3] Yes, it's harvest time for colleges and universities of the land. It's a time of change and sweat and challenge—it's time for salt and light.

And our biblical texts this day proclaim that there is salt and light. Salt cleanses and heals and preserves and seasons. Jesus has made the sacrifice to cleanse and he reaches out to us in grace to heal. He has given us his word to season our lives, and he sends his Spirit to preserve us in the faith. And what difference does it make? Well, in Peter's words, this makes us a holy nation, a chosen race, a royal priesthood: "Once you were not a people, but now you are God's people; once you had not received mercy, but now you have received mercy" (1 Peter 2:10).

How can one improve on such words of proclamation? Christ is salt for us and we are changed. No more guilt, for we are cleansed by the salt of the gospel. No more sicknesses, for we are healed by the salt of redemption. No more dullness of life, for we are seasoned by the salt of the Word. No more despair in our discipleship, for God has sent the salt of his Spirit to preserve us in the faith.

And there is light for the journey. "God is light and in him there is no darkness at all" (1 John 1:5). We have been called "out of darkness into his marvelous light" (1 Peter 2:9). This is the message we

have heard. This is the God who entered the dark places and con-
quered them. This is light of which John says, "The light shines in
the darkness, and the darkness did not overcome it" (John 1:5). This
is the news that Jesus and the disciples brought to people of many
tribes and colors and nations. And they made it a point to say and
demonstrate that salt and light were not for people who already had
it all together, but for people struggling with harvest seasons, just
like you and me. And, most important, they assured us that this salt
and this light shall endure. This salt will never slake and this light
shall not be overcome by the darkness.

We have been given salt and light in order to be people of salt
and light. We are not to hoard the salt or it will lose its power, it will
become slack. We are not to put the light under a bushel, for not
only will it not be seen—it will go out for lack of oxygen. Literally,
we have been salted down and lit up so we may be salty and light-
giving people!

So what happens when we take salt and light into the harvest
fields? The apostle Peter was in the field with flesh-and-blood harvest hands like you and me. And his counsel was very straightforward: mind your personal morals, he said, lest you lose your soul;
conduct yourself in a neighborly way with Gentiles, that is with
strangers—with people who don't share your faith or your view of
life; and be subject, he said, to the emperor and every human insti-
tution. Now that takes a little interpretation. Peter was saying don't
isolate yourselves or be obstinate about life in the community—be
a good citizen instead. In our day, as citizens of a democracy, that
means something a good deal different than it would have meant in
the first century. And finally, Peter said, live as free people and use
that freedom to live fully as servants of God. This was Peter's counsel
to people who had already passed out of death and into life, people
in their harvest season, people who were about the ministry of salt
and light.

And so we stand in the harvest fields of our lives called to be
what we already are—people of salt and light. And what would a

salty, light-filled person be like in the harvest fields of our time and place? Well, in the first place, we will make sure that we are getting steady doses of salt and light. That means staying close to the Word, being renewed by the sacraments and the discipline of prayer, and being found in the fellowship of believers.

For parents it means modeling for our children and grandchildren. While from one perspective families are one of the casualties of our culture, from another perspective they are its strength. We see it in the families of our students—the intimacy, the encouragement and the pride. And modeling parents ground their children in a sustaining faith and durable values. James Wall wrote in Christian Century, "When God drafted the Ten Commandments, He didn't conduct a market study to see what people wanted. He saw what was essential to the preservation of the human community and its connection with Him, and He set up the standards."[4] There is wisdom for parents of every age.

And in this new multi-culture that is America, there is potential for either joy or despair—joy if we find a way to both respect our differences and find our bonding unity, or despair if we emphasize our differences and ignore our common humanity. What Pope John Paul II brought to the United Nations is sanguine in this matter. He said:

> We must *overcome our fear of the future, but we will not be able to overcome it completely unless we do so together.* The "answer" to that fear is neither coercion nor repression, nor the imposition of one social "model" on the entire world. The answer is a common effort *to build the civilization of love,* founded on the universal values of peace, solidarity, justice and liberty. [5]

There is a harvest out there and it beckons salty people of light. And it isn't easy going; it's more often hard work. Ask Jeremy Torstveit of the Class of '69, a world-renowned heart surgeon who, through the Children's Heart Project, shares his gift with children who otherwise would not have a chance. Or ask last year's Cobber royalty,

Queen Kristi Rendahl who serves in the Peace Corps in Armenia, or King Ben Snell who serves with Youth Encounter Ministry in the Midwest and West Africa. Or consider the four recipients of this year's Alumni Achievement Awards—all examples of the gospel mission, living out their saltiness and sharing their light.

And there is a harvest out there for the community of faith. What should a salty, light-giving church look and act like in this harvest season? I believe the highlight of the recently completed assembly of the Evangelical Lutheran Church in America was approval of a commitment to seven initiatives for the twenty-first century. They call on us to deepen worship life; to teach the faith; to witness God's action in the world; to strengthen one another in mission; to help children; to connect with youth and young adults; and to develop leaders. It is an agenda consistent with the gospel mission; it is a salt and light agenda. As Stephen Carter, the distinguished Yale law professor tells us, we should not keep our religious ideals to ourselves. Ours is a society in need of soul, a people in need of character, a civilization seeking justice, and we have the gospel word, so let this church be salt and light to the nations.

And what will a salt- and light-filled college look like in this harvest season? At a time when church and society and especially young adults are less clear about our faith tradition, we are committed to the salt and light tasks of communicating that tradition so that students, in turn, may be both thoughtful and informed. As the attack upon scholarship grounded in faith now subsides, we are in the forefront—articulating the connections between faith and learning, connections that bring into communion the life of the mind and the life of faith. And in a period of academic deconstruction when some scholars evoke pessimism and dismiss the possibility of any grounding for truth, we affirm with good argument and confident spirit the ground of our hope, the Christ who is Lord of all, the God who is salt and light.

In a time of ambivalence about academic standards we reaffirm the calling of scholarship on this campus. There is no room for intellectual sloth among people called to love the Lord our God with all our hearts and all our souls and all our minds.

In a time when the popular arts often doggerelize culture, profane the language and pollute the human spirit, we cultivate the traditions of sacred song and verse, traditions that reveal the life-giver, give expression to human need, and inspire the vision of a peaceable kingdom. Thus, we shall be salt and light.

My friends, the field is white unto harvest. And it is sweaty business in a dusky time. But don't worry about the sweat—there is plenty of salt. And don't worry about the dusk, for Jesus will light the way. Live in the hope of the gospel—for you are a holy nation, a chosen race, a royal priesthood—God's own people.

So salty days or starry nights—God be with you always.

Amen

Life in the Christian Colony

Philippians 3:17-20

Today we are just two weeks into the new semester and there is good news and there is more good news: barely a day has passed without sunshine and cool evening breezes, beanies are under wraps and so are our cross-town rivals, the Moorhead State Dragons, and there were record tryouts for bands and choirs and orchestra—with exciting results to follow.

But there is perhaps what some may view as bad news in the mix. Two weeks into the semester some significant dates are drawing near—dates for the first exam, first paper, first speech, and the list goes on. The good news/bad news dilemma actually runs deeper than that. There is indeed good news in this new year. For you first-time Concordia Cobbers this is a new environment, there are new teachers with whom to study, new friends to enjoy, new opportunities for the future—in short, this is the chance for a new start. May you thrive on all that promises for you. For returning students the good news is a chance to build on last year's good record or to start fresh if last year was not all you had hoped for. If your choice of major or career is uncertain, here is a chance to do some more testing. If last year's friends were not all you hoped for, this year will provide opportunities to form some new relationships. And for those who teach and serve here—maybe this year we'll get organized well enough to stay current with our reading or our friendships—or maybe just the paper flow across our desks.

In this new term there is also the temptation to go back to old ways or find new ways that may be destructive. This is a place of learning and the academic agenda is the central agenda. But there will be temptations aplenty for all of us. One temptation is to intellectual sloth—to take the courses that challenge us least, to study only enough to get by, to avoid experiences or opinions contrary to our own, to opt for the video in place of the concert or Monday night football over the Monday night lecture, to delay study and preparation, to stretch the nights into mornings thereby compromising our true capacity.

This is a place of moral seriousness, not heaven on earth, but a place where the moral compass is taken seriously. But it also a place where we are tempted to cut corners ethically. You are or will be tempted to copy someone else's paper—someone from another section with another teacher. You may be tempted to crib for an exam—to violate the honor code to which we all are pledged. We will be tempted to slip into behaviors that seem fun at the moment and even in some quarters socially acceptable—but behaviors that have the potential of being destructive to us and to our implicit moral obligation to one another and to God.

This is a place in which equity and inclusiveness are explicit values. Yet we will each be tempted to spend our time only with people we know, folks very much like us in background and interest. We will be tempted to avoid people from new places, from different cultures and with different values and experiences. We will be tempted to bend into old and familiar categories of preference and stereotype. This is a place of religious seriousness—but even with the best of intentions we will each be tempted by busy schedules and new freedom to neglect spiritual reflection and development.

Today we heard a passage from Paul's letter to the Philippians. The letter was written to people Paul appreciated—they were good friends. Paul had brought them a new teaching—the Gospel of Christ—then they formed a church and made a new start in their lives and in their community. It became a community known for its witness and service to others. This was good news indeed.

The bad news was that as time passed some problems emerged. People started vying with one another for power and position. They were tempted by old religious ways such as works righteousness and the worship of idols. Still others were drawn off by destructive lifestyles. Someone once said there is nothing new under the sun and perhaps this text and our circumstances prove it. There is good news and there are new beginnings, and there can also be bad news and crooked new paths. But, if we let it, the good news can carry the day for us.

What Paul told the Philippians applies also to us—we are citizens of the commonwealth of heaven. We have been called to citizenship in God's kingdom. Noted Duke University professors Stanley Hauerwas and William Willimon put it in these words: "The church is a colony, an island of one culture in the middle of another. In baptism our citizenship is transferred from one dominion to another. . . ."[1] The mission statement of this college echoes Paul's comment on citizenship, for we are a place committed to influencing the affairs of the world by sending into society people who are citizens of, and committed to, the commonwealth of heaven.

This is not a majority agenda—it is an uncommon agenda in the universe of higher education in this world. In that sense we too are a colony in the midst of a foreign culture. And Paul's advice to the Philippians has a familiar echo: "Stand firm in the Lord" (Phil. 4:1) were his words to his friends, and the words reach down the centuries to us who share common citizenship with the Philippians, citizenship in the commonwealth of heaven. Paul did not leave his friends without support and his counsel is worth considering in this time of our new beginning. He implored his friends to feed their minds. In the fourth chapter of his letter he said this: "Whatever is true, whatever is honorable, whatever is just, whatever is pure, whatever is pleasing, whatever is commendable, if there is any excellence and if there is anything worthy of praise, think about these things" (Phil. 4:8).

American author, Josiah Gilbert Holland, wrote, "The mind grows by what it feeds on."[2] And in our vernacular Paul would say, "Feed your mind on good stuff, on honorable and lofty ideals." If we want to keep on growing as human beings then we will feed our minds on the best art and music and literature. We will feed our minds on worthy ideas and honorable values. If we feed our minds in these ways, our hearts will be gladdened and our vision expanded. But if we feed our minds on the pornographic or the near pornographic, on schlock—even nameless, pleasant schlock—our hearts will shrink and our spirits will starve. So I encourage you as Paul did his friends in Philippi, take time to feed your mind.

A second word of counsel from Paul for our time of new beginnings is this: Feed your soul. His words were, "Have no anxiety about anything, but in everything by prayer and supplication with thanksgiving let your requests be made known to God" (Phil. 4:6). In the midst of a ministry filled with healing, teaching and preaching we are told this about Jesus: "In the morning, a great while before, he rose and went out to a lonely place, and there he prayed" (Mark 1:35). Jesus took time for his soul.

One of our greatest temptations is to neglect time for our soul. There is lots of action around us, enough opportunity to lose ourselves in the crowd and to justify it very rationally. Taking time for our soul is the most difficult thing of all. But is also the most important thing. The alternative to taking time for our soul is starving it. Jesus went to that lonely place to discover God's role for him, to experience God's mercy, to discover God's power. Paul encouraged his friends to follow that example. Let us claim this special resource without which life simply is not the same.

A third word of counsel from Paul is that we take time for our neighbors. Paul implored his friends to let their gentleness be known to others, to keep on doing the things they had "learned and received and heard" from him (Phil. 4:9). This place is about service—service firmly planted in the mission statement and thoroughly institutionalized in a score of human service activities. When Jesus called his people, the members of his commonwealth of heaven, he called them to serve others in Judea, in Samaria, and in the uttermost parts of the earth. There will be opportunities to connect with people in the uttermost parts of the earth in a variety of activities on this campus, in classrooms, and through events like the coming symposium. And our first place for serving others, our Judea and Samaria, will be right here—with roommate, classmate, teammate, colleague, friend, and stranger. Here we will find opportunities aplenty to bear witness to God's love and will.

It is a season of new beginnings when the good news is in the ascendancy. We are citizens of the commonwealth of heaven, called to serve the one who is the way, the truth, and the light. We will experience good news and bad news, but through it all we have good counsel—to feed our minds, to feed our souls, to feed our neighbors. And the best news from Paul are these words: "The God of peace will be with you" (Phil. 4:9).

So be it. So be it.

Amen

And the Word Became Flesh

John 1:14-17

Let me share some stories from my childhood. My favorite uncle lived far away from my home. When he came to visit it meant good cheer, for in addition to taking time for the adults, he made time for me. He would come out to the barn to see my 4-H calves and to my room to see my 4-H ribbons. Our relationship was not just formal; it was expressed in concrete acts of recognition and care.

My favorite aunt was born in Norway. When she came to visit she always made Norwegian pancakes, lefse and fancy cookies. But what was special to me was that this Norwegian farmer's daughter would don a pair of overalls and come out to the barn and help me milk cows. She was a prized person because her affection went beyond, "Hello Paul, its good to see you again, my how you've grown." Her affection took a form that was active and real to me.

One more story—this one a Christmas Eve in the late 1930s. The family tradition was that we opened gifts on Christmas Eve at Grandma's house. Christmas was a little slim because of poor crops and poorer prices, but Grandma always came through with a knitted cap or scarf or mittens, with homemade candy and a new toy. But the weather that Christmas Eve was growing stormy so my dad set out for town to get the gifts from Grandma's house and bring them home so that we could celebrate, blizzard or not. Evening came and the weather grew worse and Dad had not returned. We were concerned about what might have happened; was he stuck in a snow bank? Or lost in the storm? Finally, at about 11:00 P.M. the horses and sleigh appeared and there was Dad, safely home—all of which made that Christmas the most special in our family's life together.

The thread that runs through these stories is that relationships turn on concrete things, in acts of love when affection takes on flesh and blood. And that leads to the words from our text: "And the Word became flesh and lived among us . . . full of grace and truth" (John 1:14). God understood our need for the concrete, and we were so important to God that he took on human form and entered into a real, concrete, flesh-and-blood relationship with us.

Concrete, flesh-and-blood experiences are important to us. We talk about experiential learning a lot here at Concordia. And people who have traveled to Europe on a May Seminar or worked as an intern in a business or student taught in a school all come back saying that the subject matter—whether business or religion, language or mathematics—became more meaningful than ever before because it was experienced in a concrete way. Isn't it so that from our earliest day until now, experience—flesh-and-blood encounters with the truth—are a superb form of leaning? Arithmetic was an abstraction, perhaps a nuisance, until I started having to keep track of my own money. Geography became real when I visited relatives in a different state—and so it goes for all of us.

God has always recognized our need for concrete, flesh-and-blood experience in his relationship to his people. The Old Testament is full of examples of God ministering in direct ways to the needs of his people. As the writer of the gospel of John reminds us, God gave Moses the law. It was not an abstraction but a declarative act to meet the needs of people wandering in the wilderness and in need of some help to serve God and one another more faithfully. God did not leave his people isolated, bereft of help, and subject to their own ruminations and abstract powers of reasoning. No, God appeared to Moses and gave the people something concrete to help them.

In this season we contemplate the coming of Christ, of God becoming flesh and blood in fulfillment of his promise. God became human—incarnation, we call it. Jesus sweat as we sweat, suffered beyond our capacity to understand, lost loved ones, had good friends and good times, and was eventually betrayed, humiliated, and turned away. Christ became one with our experience. Jesus walked the countryside; he didn't limit his appearances to the lecture circuit, and there would be no world tour. No, instead, he met people where they were. And in so doing, Christ became flesh to the needs and circumstances of people like us: he healed the sick, exorcised those possessed by evil spirits, reproved those who were self-righteous, offered a fuller life to those caught up in self-indulgence, brought comfort to those who were weary and afraid, and suggested new standards of justice for those concerned with the law.

Becoming flesh and relating to human situations was a revolutionary way of communicating the reality of God, and most people didn't approve of it or couldn't accept it. The Greeks in Christ's time regarded material things as being of low account, the prison house of the soul. As Plutarch saw it, it was nothing less than blasphemy to involve God in the affairs of the world. The early church continued to have trouble with this flesh-and-blood God. The Docetists held that Jesus was, in fact, only a phantom—his body wasn't real, he couldn't feel pain and hunger, weariness or sorrow. In contrast, the writer of John proclaimed categorically that those who deny the incarnation, this God become flesh, were on the wrong track.

"And the Word became flesh and lived among us." The historical record is clear. God became incarnate to minister to our human needs. Not content to be an abstraction, a figment of the imagination, a thesis for speculation by philosopher or theologian, scientist or poet, God became flesh.

And God becomes flesh for us today just as he did for people 2000 years ago. He is with us still, consistent with his promise to be with us always. As John put it, "from his fullness we have all received, grace upon grace" (John 1:16). God reaches out to us in our flesh-and-blood, day-by-day existence. God reaches out to an age and generation that is confused about its future. I believe it was Lutheran theologian William Lazareth who put it this way, "Never was there a time when a brilliant but broken world has been more in need of Christ. Never has there been a time when the stakes were higher and God's enemies stronger." But just as Jesus did not shrink from his enemies when he walked the earth, neither does he shrink from them now. By grace, God becomes flesh and blood with us as we live out God's call to love a broken world. God's grace reaches out to the student unsure about being a teacher or a social worker, a pastor or a business executive. The grace of God reaches out to the student in confusion about friendship, the price of approval, and the values of discipleship. God's grace reaches out so that those who are in sorrow over death and disappointment can accept the thing that they don't understand. Grace reaches out to us in our human situations today just as it did in a foreign land of shepherds and farmers, a people indentured to a foreign power 2000 years ago. God reaches out to the artist and musician, people like Paul Christiansen and Paul Allen who in each year's Christmas concert find some new expression of beauty and truth. God's grace reaches out to the student of science in the unfolding of the limitless possibilities and intricacies of life and the universe. His grace reaches out to the student who has broken a rule of life and, while not escaping the civil consequences of his action, finds peace with God. God's grace reaches out to us through others, persons who care for us as little Christs.

Yes, the word continues to become flesh and dwell among us. As we anticipate the celebration of the birth of Christ this advent season, it is with the assurance that God is with us too, caring for us, for our flesh and blood needs, making of us new creatures, giving us a mission, a sense of justice and—best of all—grace upon grace.

Redeemer, come, with us abide;
Our hearts to Thee we open wide;
Let us Thy inner presence feel;
Thy grace and love in us reveal.[1]

"Rejoice, rejoice, Emmanuel has come to us."
Amen

God's Future

Matthew 2:13-21

We begin this new semester the way we ended the old one—with wind and blowing snow and school closings left and right. All of this tests our reputation for sturdiness, forbearance and—some would say—masochism! In addition to shifting semesters in the academic year, we have shifted seasons in the church year—from Advent to Christmas and now Epiphany. There is of course continuity in the gospel story from season to season, but there are differences in emphasis. Let me talk about one of those differences today.

The Advent story and Christmas texts contain many rich themes, and one of those themes is that God has given us a future. Jesus has come into the world to fulfill the words of the prophets and the needs of humanity. He came to bring sight to the blind, healing to the sick, liberty to the slave, peace to the embattled, company to the lonely, respect to the outcast, wisdom to all seekers, and salvation to sinners. Indeed, all of us find a home somewhere in that list. The word that comes is Emanuel, God with us. In Christ, God literally gives us a future. This is the heart of the gospel story that comes to us in the Advent and Christmas seasons.

Now as we shift to Epiphany I would submit that we find new themes, and one of them is that God's future is in our hands. Let me develop this idea. In our Bible text we learn that Herod, the local political ruler and sometimes generous king, became very jealous over the news of Christ's birth, and he set out to destroy him. Herod decreed that every male child in Bethlehem and the surrounding region under the age of two should be killed. This event is often referred to as "the slaughter of the innocents." It is part of Matthew's account and not a happy story. But an angel of the Lord told Joseph to flee to Egypt with Mary and Jesus, and in that action, God would literally put Jesus' future into Joseph and Mary's hands. Once in Egypt, a city gave refuge to Joseph and Mary. Again, God was placing Jesus' future in the hands of humans—this time the Egyptian hosts.

This tradition of God's future being placed in human hands did not begin with this text. Remember Mary's pregnancy? God put Jesus' future into Mary's hands; she was responsible for nurturing a healthy fetus. How about the story of Jesus' birth? The stable owner surely got more than he bargained for in providing a home for God's Son. And the shepherds out in the fields no doubt bringing food, providing company, and passing the word? God's future was in their hands too. In Jesus' childhood there would be priests and rabbis at the temple teaching Jesus about the traditions of Yahweh. Now we believe that God is omnipotent—God can do what God wills when and where he wills it—but this text tells us that God's future was placed in human hands on many occasions.

But what about the here and now? What about us? To go back to the text, can God go it alone today or are there Herods out there intent on destroying Jesus and slaughtering the innocents, Herods who would take away our future by destroying the peace, goodwill, and justice of God, Herods who would water down the only truth that can set us free?

As we turn the calendar of the new year, it is worth revisiting God's adversaries, the Herods of the present order. God wants children to be fed. But according to the year-end report from Bread for the World, 12.4 million children will die this year due to malnutrition or preventable diseases. In America 13.6 million are hungry or at risk of hunger. There he is—Herod in our midst—and God's future is placed in our hands.

God bids us to multiply our talents both for our delight and as a form of praise. This college, this place of learning, is about that task.

But it is tempting to "fake it." Luther E. Smith, professor of theology at Emory University, said this in a convocation address to students:

> Faking it for a class session . . . is one thing. But it is so easy to find ourselves making faking it a lifestyle. We fake it with others. We fake it with ourselves. We fake it with God. This summer I saw a bumper sticker that said "Jesus is coming. Look busy!"[1]

Whenever we fake it in the classroom, whenever we slack off in our academic endeavor, whenever we compromise excellence it is a sign that Herod is in our midst slaughtering the innocents in quest of his enemy Jesus.

God bids us to tell all the nations, beginning with our neighbor, all that we have heard with our ears, seen with our eyes, and lived in our hearts. We are to be bearers of God's truth and tradition. Looked at in secular terms, this tradition is powerful. Robert Bellah, well-known philosopher of social history, points out that our morality and our democracy have powerful roots in the biblical tradition. He doesn't argue for a monolithic religious society, but he pleads with us to keep the biblical tradition alive so that it may enrich the public philosophy and personal conduct of our citizens.

Herods strike close to home. Cornelius Plantinga of Calvin College describes the seven deadly sins of contemporary society: First there is debased entertainment—people entertained by cruelty and celebrations of shamelessness. Next comes moral distancing—people living inside their comfort zones, detached witnesses to genocide, atrocities, and everyday violence. Third is the sin of addiction, especially those freely chosen. Abuse of children is next on Plantinga's list. He writes, "A father who sexually abuses his daughter corrupts her. He breaks all the little bones of self-respect that hold her character together. Filled with shame and anger, the corrupted child is extremely likely to abuse her children."[2] The fifth sin is what Plantinga calls the perversion of excellence, when people devise and defend high-minded fraud. Then there is generational selfishness, including adult children who abandon their aged parents emotionally or financially. Finally, there are the sins that keep on giving—lust, gluttony, and anger. All of these are signs that Herod is in our midst and the gospel news is under siege. In the face of these signs, to be called a Christian or a Christian college should make us very uncomfortable indeed.

The Epiphany news is that God's future is in our hands just as surely as it was in the hands of Joseph and Mary and the Egyptians 2000 years ago. The encouraging news is that God does not leave us without resources for this task. There are the gifts of intelligence and skill with which we each have been endowed, there is the company of the saints, there is the sustaining food of word and sacrament, and there is the assurance of God's Spirit in our lives. And there is the inspiring precedent of people who have accepted the responsibility for God's future: faithful Mary and Joseph; the disciples, along with Mary and Martha and family friends who accepted God's call and took the risks; and the citizens of that long-forgotten Egyptian city who were willing to jeopardize their security and good name for the sake of God's future.

There are opportunities aplenty for us to claim responsibility for God's future. Every class assignment is such an opportunity—a chance to expand our knowledge and hone our skills for appointments as yet unknown. Life in this community gives us opportunity to show friendship to the lonely neighbor, acceptance to the different one, affirmation to the uncertain soul, and justice to the besieged. Everyday we will have opportunity to care for the common life, to give witness to those core values of honesty and respect and those core virtues of fidelity and forbearance. And yes, there will be need to see and speak plainly to the Herods in our midst—the Herods of violence and selfishness, of ignorance and mediocrity, of immorality and unbelief. We will have opportunity to take responsibility for God's future by attending to the Word, by speaking the good news, and by building up the body of Christ in this place.

God used a family and a community to secure his future in the face of Herod's onslaught. There are still Herods out there and we are still called to secure God's future. In this new year may we hear that call and respond to it in lives of praise and service.

Amen

An Uncomfortable Day

Luke 20:9-18

In a recent issue of *The Christian Century,* a writer described Ash Wednesday as the most uncomfortable day of the year. It begins with the morning liturgy of the marking of ashes on the forehead, he recalled. And part of the liturgy for that rite reads, "from dust thou art, to dust thou shalt return," and with those words and the mark of an ashen cross, we are reminded—in a very visible way—of our mortality. Pretty uncomfortable stuff, indeed.

Our Bible text for this day—the parable of the unfaithful servants—presents us with still another uncomfortable image. The literal dimensions of the story are clear enough. There is the landholder who planted a fine vineyard and then rented it out and left the neighborhood. Then there were the tenants who farmed the land, who kept the vineyard. Come harvest time, when the landholder sent his servant to collect a share of the harvest, the tenants beat the servant, as well as two others subsequently sent with the same task. The landholder then sent his son to collect the rent and tenants murdered him. In his wrath, the landholder destroyed the tenants.

It is not a pretty story in its literal dimension, but as a story of faith, it becomes particularly uncomfortable. We recognize God as the landholder who created the world for the enjoyment, nourishment, and use of the tenants. Along with that, there is the expectation that as trustees of the gift, the people would serve God. But the tenants—God's people—missed that accountability dimension; indeed, they ignored it and defied it. Then God sent servants to remind them of their responsibility—we call them the prophets.

And not liking their message, the people sent the messengers on their way with a swift kick. Then God came to the people through his Son, Jesus Christ, and this time they not only ignore the message, they murder the messenger. And in the final scene God exercised the ultimate accountability and destroyed the unfaithful servants. This parable, as one interpreter has described it, is a story of unmitigated disaster. There is no "maybe," no "but," no "once upon a time" beginning or ending here.

Why does this story make us uncomfortable in our present world? For several reasons. First of all, because it confronts us on this first day of Lent with our sinfulness. It reminds us that we too are tenants. Like God's people of old, we have been given a blessing and a trust. We are expected to share the largess with others, to be a leaven in the world. But in this parable we are reminded of what we already know, that our tendency is to think we own the blessing and that it is exclusively for our use. The signs of the parable appear in my life almost daily when I dismiss the call to faithfulness as so much works righteousness. It is likewise evident in a society of individuals who think that their ultimate accountability is to themselves. And the signs of the parable in our time include churches in which stewardship peaks out at two percent or less of an average member's income.

Theologian Martin Heinecken has described some of the sins of pride that beset us. One is the sin of superior virtue in which we claim that our judgment is superior to God's when it comes to the use of our gifts. We claim to know what's best. There's no need to "wait on the Lord," we'll move ahead on our own. The apostle Paul did it in the early church with his persecution of those he determined to be God's enemies. And we do it today when we pigeon-hole the deserving and the undeserving among the poor and wretched of the earth.

Next, there is the sin of superior intellect whereby we think that we know more about the world than God did at the time of creation. We say, "Our wisdom is superior to God's wisdom," or, "We know more now than folks did thousands of years ago," and then it becomes easy to rationalize both God's will and revelation. I mean, in the days of the apostles and prophets, people didn't know about archeology and science and literary criticism so their interpretations of God's will were naïve. "I can do better than that," we think. Churches sometimes get into this box as well—particularly churches that begin to rationalize basic tenants of the faith.

The sin of superior faith in ourselves to control heaven and earth, time and eternity is next on Heinecken's list. We have faith in our ability to rearrange the environment and the atoms without fear of consequence, faith that our economic and political systems are inherently virtuous and self-correcting and faith that science will spare us from the consequences of immune deficiencies and automobiles flying across the highway uncontrolled.

And perhaps the ultimate is the sin of superior power. The tenants deliberately killed Christ; they assumed that power, the power to defy God. It sounds like some contemporary religious leaders who make deals with God to raise money. But we ourselves don't escape this sin. Who has not sometimes manipulated God and other people to his or her own ends? In sum, this parable leads each of us to confess with new earnestness the words of the liturgy, "We are in bondage to sin and cannot free ourselves."[1]

The parable makes us even more uncomfortable by confronting us with the consequences of sin. "Everyone who falls on that stone will be broken to pieces," reads Luke 20:18. And no extenuating circumstances are noted in the text. Judgment, destruction, and death are the consequences of sin. Ash Wednesday may be for us the most uncomfortable day of the year because it confronts us with our sin and our ultimate accountability. Ashes are not a thing of beauty—they are gray and greasy and contaminating. Clearly, we are called by this day and by this text to recall in a vivid way our condition.

But, friends in Christ, while this may be the most uncomfortable day of the church year, it is not the only day of the church year. We are called by this day and this liturgy and this text to repentance.

It is appropriate to be uncomfortable with our sin—but not with our God. And even on this day we may anticipate other days—days of reconciliation, resurrection and glory. Because we can anticipate those other days, in a special way this day calls us to faith—not faith in sin, but faith in God whose promises are sure and whose mercy is beyond our understanding. So sure are those promises and so generous is that mercy that tenants like us can expect to be renewed each day, thus enabled to live out our vocations in God's vineyard.

Amen

Bargaining with God

Exodus 34:1-10

The story of the rebellion of the Israelites, the epic of the golden calf, may be worth recounting for it both sets the scene for our biblical text today and reveals some important truths about our human condition, truths worthy of consideration in this penitential season. The bare bones of the story are that Moses, the leader of God's chosen people, went to the mountain to speak with God. God provided extended instruction and finally gave him "two tablets of the covenant, tablets of stone, written with the finger of God" (Exod. 31:18).

All of this took considerable time, some forty days according to the text, which in the symbolic language of scripture may have been a very long time. The people grew restless in Moses' absence for they were without structure and without Moses' leadership. Aaron had been left in charge but he had grown dispirited. It had been a wonderful ride for the Israelites under Moses' leadership—lots of action, plenty of supernatural feats, but now he was gone and there was no action, no recent miracles of food or deliverance. And so, Aaron decided, "Let's try some of the old action. We'll collect the gold jewelry in the camp; we'll melt it and mold it into a golden calf." The calf was an object familiar from the Israelites' former life, a symbol of fertility, vitality and energy.

At Aaron's instruction the people collected all the gold, melted it, and made a golden calf. And they celebrated, just as they had in former times. With eating and drinking and dancing they dedicated their new symbol. Pretty small stuff in the big picture? Maybe so.

But what they did next was to really turn the page—they worshiped and sacrificed to the golden calf. Moses had promised new things and claimed that he talked with God himself, but Moses was gone and there had been no recent revelations. The people needed something to believe in, to cling to, so they said, "Let's go back to the old gods. When Moses is away we Israelites will play!"

One day Moses finally came back from the mountain and he was steamed. He threw the two tablets of stone on which were inscribed the Ten Commandments, broke them at the foot of the mountain. Then he took the golden calf, burned it with fire, ground it to powder, scattered it on the water, and made the Israelites drink it. Then he confronted Aaron whom he had left in charge and asked for a full account. Aaron, chagrined and caught red-handed said, "Not me, Moses, these folks did it! They grew restless in your absence and so I said, 'Take off your gold,' and they did. I threw it in the fire and presto, out comes this calf. I mean, Moses, these people made me do it and I'm really innocent of any wrongdoing here."

And Moses burned with anger and there was an accounting. The sons of Levi were set loose and blood was spilled on the ground that day; about 3000 fell. What Moses did was an expression of what God felt when he said, "I have seen this people, how stiff-necked they are. Now let me alone, so that my wrath may burn hot against them and I may consume them" (Exod. 32:9-10). This was no slap on the wrist discipline, no days off for good behavior, no suspended sentence. God's intention was judgment—total, final, and all-encompassing—fire and dust and blood!

Now how do we find our place in this story—this old, old story? I suggest that we all journey in wilderness times. There is the wilderness of uncertain health. Two weeks ago I visited with two Cobbers in Arizona, both in treatment for cancers that are unrelenting and, sad to say, their son—in the fullness of life—battles a terminal cancer of his own. There is also the wilderness of relationships within families. I think of two parents with whom I visited some years ago. Their son violated children and the parents were left to wonder why.

And then there is the wilderness of false gods and idolatry that can trip up people looking for a larger cause, a meaningful life, a durable commitment.

There is anxiety in the wilderness and it leads people to offer up gods of their own construction. The god may be as innocent as physical fitness or as destructive as anorexia. The god we choose may be the self-destructiveness of Kevorkian, the self-indulgence of chemistry, the self-delusion of brand X, or the self-consumption that depletes the soil, pollutes the air and poisons the water. And some may choose to measure out their gold for calves of brass and glass—or one hundred thousand dollar Hummers.

Once we discover that such gods have failed us we, like Aaron, are quick to shift the blame. "My good friends were doing it so what was I supposed to do?" "I'm under a lot of stress and I was pushed over the edge." "What's my business is my business and as long as I don't hurt anyone, what does it matter?" We are living in the therapeutic age, quick to rationalize error and explain away evil. If "no fault" is a good idea in the insurance business, then why not also in the living of life? Which of us in our respective wildernesses has not made a bad choice or two or more along the way?

When we take account of our wilderness journeys, then we may find ourselves in Aaron's story. Taken at the telling thus far, there is no comfort, no encouragement. Only fire and dust and blood, for God was angry. He threatened to destroy all the people and then have Moses start over again with a new gang. Moses, bearing the cross of his calling amidst these disobedient and unruly people, might have said, "Just fine, God, do it!" But instead, he implored God:

> Turn from your fierce wrath; change your mind and do not bring disaster on your people. Remember Abraham, Isaac, and Israel, your servants, how you swore to them by your own self, saying to them, "I will multiply your descendants like the stars of heaven, and all this land that I have promised I will give to your descendants, and they shall inherit it forever." (Exod. 32:12-13)

Thus did Moses plead with God. And then the text reads, "The Lord changed his mind about the disaster that he planned to bring on his people" (32:14).

The beautiful words of the text read thus:

> "The Lord, the Lord, a God merciful and gracious, slow to anger, and abounding in steadfast love and faithfulness, keeping steadfast love for the thousandth generation, forgiving iniquity and transgression and sin, yet by no means clearing the guilty, but visiting the iniquity of the parents upon the children and the children's children to the third and fourth generation." (Exod. 34:6-7)

We each live out the reality of God's experience with the Israelites. And we live out the promises, indeed the very nature of God. We each live with our own temptations in the wilderness, and we too may scapegoat some god when we are called into account. We often experience the consequences of our wilderness choice: there is the death of the innocents, the pain of betrayed relationships, the awful guilt of the harm we have caused, the shame of untended obligations, and the pollution of our body politic and our planet earth. Yes there may be fire and dust and blood—even to the third and fourth generations.

But God heard Moses' plea and God changed his mind. God changed his mind at the simple and sincere petition of a human being. And God not only spared this unruly people, God also made a covenant with them. God promised them his presence and his providence: "I hereby make a covenant. Before all your people I will perform marvels, such as have not been performed in all the earth or in any nation; and all the people among whom you live shall see the work of the Lord; for it is an awesome thing that I will do with you." (Exod. 34:10). And God gave them a set of commandments with which they were able to shape a civil and faithful life. God the promise keeper would send Jesus the Christ, thus renewing the covenant. God continues to do awesome things in our lives, in our communities and in our world.

Our life journey may not be as painful as it was for Aaron and the Israelites, but in any case, we have an advocate in Christ, the law to give us direction, and the promises of God—promises of forgiveness and love to the thousandth generation.

Amen

To Be Continued

Psalm 19:1-10; Ephesians 2:8-10; Matthew 5:1-14

When I grew up in small town America, the local movie theatre always had a Saturday matinee for kids. One feature of the matinee was a serial, a story told in weekly installments—a practice designed to keep us coming back for more. One never knew how many installments there would be in a serial but when you saw the tag line "to be continued" you knew there would be at least one more. That was always frustrating for a farm kid like me who only rarely attended the Saturday matinee.

The Easter narrative is another of those serial stories. This time it is the story of God's future. The resurrection is our tagline that the story was not over at the cross; it is "to be continued." Beyond that, we are called and enabled to be part of the continuing story, both individually and as members of this Concordia community.

Today I share with you three premises in search of a conclusion, a conclusion that is finally "to be continued." There is plenty of documentation for the reality that God is at work and that is premise one. The psalm of the day speaks in the present tense: "The law of the Lord is perfect, reviving the soul; the decrees of the Lord are sure, making wise the simple" (Ps. 19:7). There are no past tenses here. And the reality of this present tense God is displayed before our very eyes as winter turns to spring. In April we see green grass, a sort of miracle but an assurance that God is at work again.

The biblical narrative is full of evidence of God's continuing revelatory and creative work. The Israelites experienced it and were shaped by it. And in the first century God appeared again, healing, inspiring, teaching, cajoling. And when his Son completed his earthly journey, then God sent his Spirit—no doubt about that when the tongues of people and the tongues of fire were made manifest in Jerusalem.

In the present time we see evidence—but clearly not all of it—that God continues his healing and reconciling work in the world. We see it when peace is restored in a family or in a whole community, as we have witnessed in recent days as friends and loved ones rallied around missionary David Simonson in a time of physical crisis and as this whole region rallied around the family of Dru Sjodin at her disappearance.[1,2] God assures us that the future is in his hands. We have God's promise of a new heaven and a new earth. We have God's promise to be with us in every condition. We have God's promise to wipe away every tear. We hear some of God's promises in one of the texts of the day—promises to bless the peacemakers, the meek, the merciful, the pure in heart, and those who seek righteousness. And we have Christ's own words that we "will be" his witnesses.

My second premise is that the future God has in store does not depend on us. Paul was upfront about this when he assured the Ephesians that it was by grace that they were saved through faith—not through their own works. Martin Luther put his spin on this idea in his explanation of the Second Petition of the Lord's Prayer, which says, "Thy kingdom come." Of it, Luther wrote, "To be sure, the kingdom of God comes of itself, without our prayer."[3] The future God has in store comes without our action; in fact, it is hidden from us. Jesus told the disciples at his ascension, "It is not for you to know the times or periods that the Father has set by his authority" (Acts 1:7). That can be frustrating for fundamentalists who want it all laid out and assume that it is, or for rationalists like most of us who think we may find a way to master the universe. The record of both fundamentalists and rationalists proves the point.

Premise three is that we can all be part of God's "to be continued" future. God's future doesn't depend on us but we can be part of it. Paul's words to the Ephesians put it very succinctly, "For we are what [God] has made us, created in Jesus Christ for good works, which God prepared beforehand to be our way of life" (Eph. 2:10).

A commentary on this text by Pheme Perkins of Boston College put it this way, "These works are not burdensome commandments but an appropriate response to the extraordinary salvation already extended to us by God."[4] In his explanation of the Third Petition of the Lord's Prayer, Martin Luther wrote, "To be sure, the good and gracious will of God is done without our prayer, but we pray in this petition that it may also be done by us."[5]

These premises lead me to the conclusion that while neither you nor I nor this college is in charge of the coming of God's kingdom, we are called to be part of it. And to this calling we bring special gifts and special responsibilities. The gifts are manifest among us: there are the special gifts of the Christian and Lutheran traditions that provide a substantive foundation for our understanding of God's world and God's will for it and us. We have the gift of community where kindred hearts are joined in common endeavor. This is a place to experience and live out our interdependence. It is a community whose citizenship extends well beyond the campus. There is the gift of learning and the opportunities it provides to explore the delights of creation, the possibilities of human understanding and will. And finally, there is the gift of praise—the opportunity to give thanks to God for infinite grace and boundless opportunity.

And with these special gifts come special challenges for those who wish to be part of the coming of God's kingdom. For example, there is the challenge of maintaining our identity as a Lutheran Christian college in a world of many faiths and cultures, maintaining that identity and then reaching out so that we may be in common cause with brothers and sisters of other faiths and traditions. There is the challenge of reforming a calcifying church that is the victim of the secularization by which it has been shaped. There is the challenge of relating to a global church in the Southern Hemisphere with different agendas than ours. And how shall we relate to a culture that stresses immediacy and superficial reality, a culture that erodes civilizing values and virtues? There is an opportunity to serve a new generation of students, a generation of seekers who are looking for some reliable truths amidst the plethora of theories and practices that typify modernity. There is the challenge to invigorate the commitment of this community and the church universal to equity, justice, and inclusiveness.

This is, in some sense, a chapel farewell for me since I will soon complete my service. Not many have the privilege of a second farewell homily so I take this opportunity to reassure and challenge you in this second leaving.[6] The reassurance is that God's work among you continues. And God's future like your own future does not depend on you. That is what Easter tells us. And God's future may not always be entirely clear to you; there will be ambiguities and sidetracks and all the rest. But God has prepared work for you and invites you to sign on, to be part of God's future, a story "to be continued."

We are called to care for one other and for the church and, indeed, the whole world with all the energy and intellect we can muster. And we have the energy and intellect to give in this place as we chart a new course. Think of the potentially creative synergies between and among our mission, our tradition, our vocation, our academic goals, and our curriculum. We have energy and intellect to give as we imagine and implement new ways of modeling and expressing our citizenship responsibility in the earthly kingdom. We have energy and intellect to give as we develop ways to insure that every student has an opportunity to be fully engaged in the life of this community from orientation through first year through commencement and then into life as an alumna/alumnus of the college. We have energy and intellect to give as we discover the academic richness of this community and channel it in ways that will enhance our capacity to serve our students better in the future. We have such energy and intellect to join in the coming of the kingdom, the story of God's work.

I began by recalling the matinee serial and its tagline "to be continued." So it is with God's work among us—it is a story that is to be continued. God has given us the gifts, the opportunity and the call to be part of his continuing story. So *carpe diem*, seize the day, seize the opportunity with all your intellect and energy.

Amen

Mass of Exodus

Exodus 3:1-2, 7, 10-12; Ruth 1:15-18; John 20:24-27

When I walked out of Concordia's Memorial Auditorium on my graduation day, it was raining. No chance for outdoor picture taking so I wandered back inside. Mom and Dad and Uncle Odin and Aunt Mary and especially Mardy were there and we took pictures all around. Mardy and I would be married a day later, and two weeks after that we would head off to an unknown place to begin graduate school. We were uncertain about many things but anxious about only a little, for we had our love for each other and the supporting encouragement and confidence of our friends and family going for us—they were the wind beneath our wings.

Tonight I want to share the stories of three biblical people who were on journeys to new places or unknown places. In Egypt there lived a captive people and in their midst God called a man named Moses to be their leader. "Who me?" said Moses. "Yes, you," said God. "I have chosen you, a man of confidence and strength, a man of cunning and great talent. I have chosen you to do a mighty thing and I will be with you. You will lead my people out of a land of bondage into a land of opportunity."

Moses the robust, the man of faith; God would choose him and use him. But leading the Israelites would be no sweet deal. They would rebel and test Moses time after time. Yet Moses, robust man, doer of mighty deeds, would lead them. When they cried out hungry, he made sure there was food—manna in the desert morning. When their foes would overtake them, Moses was the master campaign strategist. When the water of Marah was bitter, he threw a piece of wood in the water and it became sweet to the taste. And when the people became unruly, Moses became lawgiver and judge. Moses the robust one, full of talent and energy and ambition. Consider his epitaph: "Never since has there arisen a prophet in Israel like Moses, whom the Lord knew face to face" (Deut. 34:10).

God and Moses had frequent conversations—even arguments—in Egypt, in the Canaan Desert, and on the Sinai Mountain. But in every place on the Exodus journey, God was the wind beneath his wings.

Next, consider the story of Ruth—Ruth the faithful one. Ruth's mother-in-law Naomi was left without a husband. Then her two married sons died. Her future looked dim, her prospects almost nonexistent. She told her daughters-in-law, Orpah and Ruth, to look out for themselves, to head to their homelands where they might have a chance to survive. Hearing this advice, Orpah kissed Naomi goodbye and took leave, but Ruth, we are told, clung to Naomi. And with these beautiful words she pledged to be faithful to her: "Do not press me to leave you or to turn back from following you! Where you go, I will go; Where you lodge, I will lodge; your people shall be my people, and your God my God" (Ruth 1:16).

Ruth set out on a journey, not to a new place but to a new responsibility. She would live with Naomi, finding food and giving care. And one day she would marry again, this time to Boaz, and she would bear a child and become the great grandmother of David the prophet, poet king. Faithful Ruth, symbol of God's love—she was the wind beneath Naomi's wings. She was God's person, doing God's thing in giving care to another.

Robust Moses. Faithful Ruth. . . . Doubting Thomas.

Thomas, like the other disciples in their post-Easter journey, was scared. More than that, he was doubtful. He needed proof: "Unless I see the mark of the nails in his hands, and put my finger in the mark of the nails and my hand in his side, I will not believe" (John 20:25). And Jesus, knowing Thomas's need, reached out. For what must have been the seventh time or seven times the seventh time, he reached out to Thomas—first by extending a word of peace, then by inviting him to see the wound, to put his hand in it, and then he showed his confidence in Thomas by calling him to a new journey, a journey of ministry. And the word is that Thomas would be the one who brought the gospel to India. Undergirding all of this was Jesus' promise that wherever the talented man would go, Jesus would be there too. He would be the wind beneath Thomas's wings.

The eagle flies at speeds and over distances that defy the physics of its own body. It does so by catching the currents, riding the winds. And the eaglet, new from the nest, is carried along by the wind that is created by the parent eagle—it is literally the wind beneath its wings.

Are you a robust Moses, a woman of talent, a man of courage, a person of vision and confidence? Then know that God has called you to lead his people and that God promises to be with you on your exodus journey to a destination still unknown. God will be the wind beneath your wings.

Or are you a bearer of others' burdens, faithful and well-doing? Then God calls you to serve the sick, the homeless, the lowly, the castoffs. Whether you are Scott or Heidi, you're called to be a faithful Ruth, and even in dark days and in the presence of your enemies, God will be with you. God may surprise you as he surprised Ruth with unexpected joy. God will be the wind beneath your wings.

Or perhaps you are a Thomas, not quite sure who God is or what this cross means. Maybe you wrestle with God like Jacob or test God like the Israelites or betray God like Peter—all of which would put you in company with Thomas. Remember, God was there for Thomas and his first word was a word of peace. God's second word was a word of respect for the doubt, the third word was "Go, spread the word" and the last word was "I will go with you, I am the wind beneath your wings."

So on commencement day take your exodus journey. You will be going from this familiar place to an unknown place. You go with great gifts: the gift of robustness, the gift of faithfulness, maybe the gift of doubt. And you go with the support of this company of Cobbers—your friends, your mentors, and your pastors. You go with a calling to use your gifts, agape style; you go from this place with a word of peace in the midst of sorrow or joy or uncertainty.

And you go with God's promise, a promise as sure and as real as the bread and the wine we now share. That promise: "I will be with you. I am the wind beneath your wings."

Amen

Apocalypse Now

Malachi 4:1-2a; 2 Thessalonians 3:6-13; Luke 21:5-19

This is the changing of the seasons. One sign of that is that the high school football season is over. Have you noticed that with the play-off system all but the best team end their seasons by losing? It is also the end of the fall season—the sun is lower in the sky, the days are shorter, and the nights cooler and longer. On the church side of things we are approaching the end of the church year. Pentecost is nearly over and the texts of these days are texts about the last days, the end times. As Malachi puts it, "See, the day is coming, burning like an oven" (Mal. 4:1). Apocalypse, apocalypse now!

There are signs around us of apocalypse. In the Sudan severe famine now threatens to kill tens of thousands. It is carefully manip-ulated by the government, and according to Dan Effie, coordinator for Central Africa of Norwegian People's Aid, it is akin to ethnic cleansing. It is, in fact, a religious war raged by fundamentalist Mus-lims against the Christian population. In desperation, many are killing their cows—their only sustainable source of food, their last "insurance" policy.

In the global scheme of things our population is expected to dou-ble in the next century while our water supply will remain constant. Wally N'dow of Gambia, former Secretary General of the Second United Nations Conference on Human Settlements, predicts that in the next fifty years we will go to war over water just as in the past fifty years we have gone to war over oil. Apocalypse, apocalypse deferred.

On the American scene we mourn over our crisis of values. Political scientist James Q. Wilson writes that we now suffer from the elevation of self-expression over self-control and the wreckage is around us in the form of broken promises, broken relationships, and shattered lives. Our public life, life in community and self-government, lies on the brink of its own shattering. We do well to recall that when the founders of this republic talked about "life, liberty, and the pursuit of happiness" they did not conceive of happiness in individual terms but in relationship to the good of the neighbor. As contemporary social critic Steven Carter has put it, "Democracy doesn't provide the freedom to do what we would like . . . but rather the freedom to do what is right."[1] But we have trouble with that so in the election just past we were again the objects of attack ads in the name of the pragmatic and partisanship in matters of the common good. Perhaps it is a sign of apocalypse when our economics becomes disconnected from our politics. We focus more on "what" than on "why," on "will it work?" rather than "is it right?" and our politics has ceased to provide ethical criteria for our economics.

The church must face its own signs of apocalypse. Theologian Timothy Lull believes that the affluence of North American churches has become an obstacle to outreach. We tend to be in comfortable places looking out for ourselves and others like us. The center of action in the church has shifted from North America and Europe and the so-called mainline. Indeed, Third World nations are now sending missionaries to Europe and America and para-church structures collect more money for mission work than traditional denominations.

And for some apocalypse is neither far off nor abstract. Apocalypse is now in the form of a dreaded diagnosis, an irretrievable relationship, a betrayed trust or the imminent loss of livelihood.

How then shall we deal with the signs of apocalypse in this time and place? It is tempting to deal with it by simply conforming to the age. In the fifth century BC the Israelites saw that the evildoers were prospering so they decided to slack off in their zeal for Yahweh and the holy and faithful life. Some people respond to apocalypse now by following false teachers. Every year a few folks prophesy the end of the world. They go off half-cocked, some even destroying themselves in the process, thinking that they are messengers of God. Such people give the texts of the day a bad name. In the gospel Jesus warns, "Beware that you are not led astray" (Luke 21:8) by false teachings or by what some think of as apocalyptic events such as the destruction of the temple in Jerusalem.

But most of us are in no danger of overreacting to talk of apocalypse. We are like the Israelites in some ways—we see the good times, the material and scientific and technological progress of the centuries and we assume that there will be no apocalypse now or in the future. We have, like the Israelites, conformed to the prevailing worldview. Now neither Malachi nor Jesus provide much comfort to us. Jesus warned that people of the cross would be arrested and persecuted, betrayed, and even martyred.

Some respond to the prospect of an apocalypse by staying on the sidelines, letting the world go by and laying down the shovel and the cross. That is what Paul found among the Thessalonians—people who were so intrigued with the promises of paradise that they forgot about their present obligations as disciples. As the saying goes, they were so heavenly minded that they were of no earthly good. Paul condemned their inaction as a form of heresy, a denial of the covenant that God had made with them in Christ.

Still others respond to the prospect of apocalypse now with fear—stark panic—a helpless grief that destroys hope and life in the here and now. Many of us have experienced it when the diagnosis is given, the divorce is granted, the layoff is announced, the relationship is ended, or the betrayal is revealed—then fear is a stark, real thing. Jesus understood that. He spoke directly about it when he said, "Do not be terrified. . . ." (Luke 21:9). Do not be terrified. We have a God who understands terror and in today's gospel he assures us that he is there with us.

But, you say, if apocalypse now is not to be avoided, not to be denied, not to be explained away and not to be feared, then what? There are at least three words of counsel in these texts. The first word of counsel is that we should live out our commission. Jesus told his interrogators—some friendly, most perhaps not—that they were to live out their discipleship even in the face of the worst that life could offer. And Paul said that Christians must carry their own weight in the community. Doing justice and caring for the members of the body of Christ were expected. Paul cited his own example. He didn't sponge off anyone; he made tents and he contributed to the common treasury. And as he would later point out to the Corinthians, he passed on to others the faith he had received and urged them to do likewise.

So we are called to live out our commission, to do it at home, in the congregation and in the community. To do it by sharing our person, our dollars, and our talents with those in need and with those who have not experienced the good news of God's love in Christ. With respect to our life in community, author and relationship expert Steven Carter writes, "The key to reconstructing civility . . . is for all of us to learn anew the virtue of acting with love toward our neighbors. Love of neighbor has long been a tenet of Judaism and Christianity, and the revival of civility in America will require a revival of all that is best in religion as a force in our public life."[2]

The second word of counsel for people who would carry the cross is that they should expect adversity. Paul talked about arrest and persecution, about families and communities turning against you, and about interrogation, persecution, and martyrdom. And we know what happened to Stephen and Paul and Peter and James the son of Zebedee and thousands of others. And we know what is happening today to Christians in the Sudan.

Most of us will not have to pay for our discipleship with our lives. But if we take the problem of homelessness seriously, it may cost us some of our respectability. If we take those who are sick and dying seriously, we may have to deal with our feelings. If we take stewardship seriously, it may cost us a change in our standard of living. If we take inequality seriously, it may lead us into the conflict of life in the public square. If we take mission outreach seriously, it may create a ruckus in the congregation or in the synod. And if we take values seriously, it may make us the odd-one-out in our peer group.

The third word from these texts is that whatever apocalypse we may face, we can count on God. Jesus told his disciples that he would be with them always. More than that, they weren't even to prepare for persecution in advance because, he said, "I will give you words and a wisdom that none of your opponents will be able to withstand or contradict" (Luke 21:15). Furthermore, he assured them, "not a hair of your head will perish. By your endurance you will gain your souls" (Luke 21:18). Recall Paul's eloquent words of counsel in his letter to the Romans:

> For I am convinced that neither death, nor life, nor angels, nor rulers, nor things present, nor things to come, nor powers, nor height, nor depth, nor anything else in all creation, will be able to separate us from the love of God in Christ Jesus our Lord. (Rom. 8:38)

And if there is doubt about any of this, look at the evidence of such faith. See the evidence in an enduring church that has experienced schisms on the inside and persecution from the outside. Look at the positive signs in the remarkable grace of Kim Dae-Jung, eighth President of the Republic of Korea who spent years in prison, survived numerous attempts on his life, and on his inaugural day promised that he would not tolerate political retaliation of any kind. Look to the work of the Truth in Reconciliation Commission in South Africa. Look at the growing numbers of young people who commit time and talent to meeting the concrete, here-and-now needs of the poor and neglected. Look into the hearts of those who face death with hope and uncertainty with confidence and you will see a God who keeps his promises.

It is the changing of the seasons and apocalypse is in the air, but we have a calling and a faithful God. He promises to give us words and wisdom and he assures us that not even the gates of hell will prevail against us. Thanks be to God.

Amen

PART THREE

Elements of Faith

First Things

Faith is a gift. It comes first, and from it flow other gifts. One thinks, for example, of the fruit of the Spirit identified by Paul in his letter to the Galatians. The selections that follow concern several of the core gifts of faith: forgiveness, grace, freedom and truth, reconciliation, hope, refuge, and vocation.

In a world that is built and run on material values and "provable" assumptions, it is often hard to discern and appreciate such unseen gifts as these. Perhaps Martin Luther had it right: faith is permitting ourselves to be seized by the things we do not see. And it is in contemplation and prayer that the Holy Spirit of God seizes us and brings such gifts.

There is a lot of random "noise" in today's culture and plenty of alluring gods that promise much but deliver little. In contrast, the Christian message comes gently, delivers gracefully and guides faithfully even in the dark valleys. It has the power to change lives, to bring justice and to pursue mercy. Thanks be to God.

Forgiveness

Genesis 50:15-21; Matthew 19: 21-35

Who has not seen Andrew Lloyd Webber's *Joseph and the Amazing Technicolor Dreamcoat*? Since its original production in the early 1990s, this popular musical has played to millions. It's the story of Joseph and his eleven brothers who were jealous of Joseph's standing as the most favored son of their father, Jacob. So they sold him into slavery, then lied to their father that he was dead and went on with their lives.

But Joseph, sold into slavery, did well—winning his freedom and becoming an interpreter of dreams to the Pharaoh. And one day when his brothers were in trouble, guess who would rescue them? Good old Joseph.

The theme of the musical focuses on Joseph and his dream coat and his ability to translate dreams. It's all about magic and imagination—"Any dream will do" goes the theme song, "Any dream will do." Given the state of biblical literacy these days, some may believe that Webber's musical was the source used by the writer of the book of Genesis and today's Old Testament text.

But there are some fundamental differences between the musical and the biblical account. While the theme of the musical is about dreaming and dream coats, the unifying theme in the Genesis story and our gospel text from Matthew is forgiveness—not magic and not dreaming.

But before we can fully grasp what today's texts have to say about forgiveness, we need to put it into proper context. To do that, we need to first understand what the texts say about guilt and about vengeance. The eleven brothers of Joseph who had sold him into slavery knew about guilt. When they were eventually discovered by Joseph, they—in guilt—expected the worst. So also did the master in the parable from Matthew 19. He owed a debt that was unimaginable, perhaps something like a billion dollars in today's money. In any case, it was a larger debt than the master could ever repay to his king. And he knew that he was guilty of defrauding his king. So like Joseph's eleven brothers, he too—in guilt—was full of fear.

We know all about guilt too. Which of us has not or does not idolize someone or something higher than God—perhaps money, or fame, or power, or popularity, or an artificial high? Who has not lied to a friend or betrayed a friendship? Who has not disobeyed the command to love our neighbor? And what few of us have not despoiled the environment or ignored the weak?

Episcopal priest John Claypool wrote that we are all value-cherishing creatures. That is, certain principles and ideals are important to us. We can't violate them and go away untouched. But how do we deal with such guilt? One typical response is vengeance. While the Joseph account is a bit ambiguous about Joseph's internal feelings when he was re-united with his brothers, it was probably vengeance. The Matthew text tells a story of the second servant who owed a small debt to the first servant. In response to his plea for mercy, the first servant had him thrown into jail—vengeance. The king who initially had forgiven the first servant a huge, astronomical debt was so offended that he threw him into jail too—more vengeance. And Peter in asking if he should forgive someone who had offended him as many as seven times—what he was really saying was that, at some point, vengeance might be appropriate. Consider the relatively recent practice in our judicial system whereby the friends and family of the victims of capital crimes are given opportunity to testify in the sentencing phase of a trial. Typically, their words are words of vengeance.

Now, vengeance is not the only response to guilt. Repression is another, often surfacing in anxiety and physical and emotional pain.

Relativizing the guilt by saying "everybody's doing it" is another—but right and wrong can't be determined by popular vote. Self-punishment is still another strategy. Soren Kierkegaard's father cursed God as a lad and he never recovered in spite of his good works on the one hand and his self-flagellation on the other. You get the idea—guilt has its prodigy, inescapable and inestimable.

So our scripture texts are not about dreams and dream coats but about guilt and vengeance. But, thanks be to God, the core of these texts is about forgiveness. I am not speaking here of the forgiveness of "I'll forgive you if you'll forgive me"—that's the law of tit for tat repackaged. Neither is it the forgiveness that Joseph's brothers imagined when they said, "if you'll forgive us, then we will be your servants." And it's not the forgiveness of the master who said "you'll be free only when you've paid your debt in full" or the forgiveness Peter imagined when he suggested forgiving a person seven times—for keeping count is not the same as forgiveness. Finally, it's not the forgiveness of "now you owe me"—as though forgiveness is money in the bank to be collected later.

No, this is forgiveness so lavish and unconditional as to be unimaginable. That's what Jesus meant when he responded to Peter by saying one should forgive another not seven times but seventy times seven—an unimaginable number. And it's what Jesus pointed to in the parable when the king forgave a debt past recounting. It's what Joseph did when, the second time around, he wept at his brothers' fear and trembling. It's what the prodigal's father did as he ran to meet his son. It's what the employer did who paid the eleventh hour workers the same as the first hour workers. It is our God who says "though your sins are like scarlet, they shall be like snow" (Isa. 1:18). And again, "As far as the east is from the west, so far he removes our transgressions from us" (Ps. 103:12).

So wherever you are at today, whatever you may harbor in the deep places of your soul—God invites you to his table with the lavish, sustainable promise: the gracious forgiveness of all your sins, in the name of the Father, and of the Son, and of the Holy Spirit.

There's one more word here that Andrew Lloyd Webber missed—the word is restoration. It's what happened when Joseph told his brothers that they would enjoy care and safety—they and their children. It's what happened to the servant in the parable when freed of his massive, uncountable debt. Its what happened when the prodigal son was restored. Its what happened when the blind gained sight and Zaccheus' life was turned around.

Jesus bids those who are restored by his gift of forgiveness to turn things around for others—that they too may be restored. It's what he told Peter to do: "Forgive others," he said, "and unconditionally." It was Christ who taught us to pray, "forgive us our trespasses as we forgive those who trespass against us."

It is often not easy to forgive. We usually want to see who will make the first move—it's back to reciprocity again—a kind of conditional forgiveness. In the *Merchant of Venice*, Shakespeare put it this way, "How shalt thou hope for mercy, rendering none."

Most of us need a change of heart that God, by his Spirit, promises to each of us. A promise that we literally eat and drink at our Lord's Table. Once received, that promised forgiveness becomes the beginning of restoration for both the forgiven and the forgiver. And such forgiveness is not a game changer—it's a life changer. We come away free, without the burdens of guilt or vengeance. We come away loved by a God who promises to stay with us no matter what. We come away with hope for God is at work in the world, in this community of faith and in our lives. We have God's word on that.

Amazing grace!

Amen

Hope

1 Peter 3:15-16

The presidential inauguration recently past recalls for me the stirring words of an earlier inauguration, that of John F. Kennedy in 1961:

> Now the trumpet summons us again—not as a call to bear arms, though arms we need—not as a call to battle, though embattled we are—but a call to bear the burden of a long twilight struggle, year in and year out, "rejoicing in hope, patient in tribulation"—a struggle against the common enemies of man: tyranny, poverty, disease, and war itself. . . .
>
> Ask not what your country can do for you, but what you can do for your country.[1]

These were inspiring, hopeful words. And the response from across the nation to this president who had been elected by the narrowest of margins was bipartisan and warm and even adoring. But by the end of the decade of the 1960s the high hopes had been dashed by the trauma of assassinations and the agony of the long and controversial war in Vietnam.

In the face of life's injustices, immorality, and bondage it is small wonder that people flee from such hope to what appears to be the secure or familiar ground of self or cynicism or ideological rigidity. And that is how the social scientists read the career choices of the young, the political indifference of the majority, and the confusing claims of the religious. Against this backdrop consider the call of scripture: "Always be ready to make your defense to anyone who demands from you an accounting for the hope that is in you"

(1 Peter 3:15). Now hope is something we all talk about: hope for a break in the weather, hope for a good job or a good grade. But what of the hope referred to in this text? What kind of hope is it? Is it different from hoping for a good grade or a balanced budget or a shelter for the homeless? The epistle writer was writing to a people who had endured a good deal of persecution. He was speaking to them of the hope we have in Christ, so let's look at the Christian tradition and the concept of hope that it entails.

First, we discover that our hope is not based on human will or capacity but on divine, transcendent action. It is a hope based on resources beyond us—the God of Abraham, Isaac, and Jacob. This is in contrast to hope based solely on the human will and capacity to do good things. That is, it is hope with a transcendent source. We just celebrated the birthday of Martin Luther King Jr. and will soon celebrate the birthday of Abraham Lincoln—both were inspired by such transcendent hope as this.

Our hope is also distinguished because it is based on a God who loves us with infinite mercy. The fragility and failure that characterize the ordinary brands of hope do not change God's attitude of love toward us. Martin Luther King had his human weaknesses and Abraham Lincoln was plagued by haunting bouts of depression—and God loved both of them through it all.

Another distinguishing quality of the hope that is in us is that it is based on the God who is active in the world, renewing it and redeeming it. This is evidenced in the life, death, and resurrection of Christ and in the reality of God's continuing activity in reconciling the world. It is in that context that we can interpret Martin Luther King's ability to touch the conscience of the nation and inspire a moral crusade. And that enables us to understand how Abraham Lincoln, living in a world of hard military and political choices, could act out of courage and vision.

So the hope that Peter spoke about and the kind that King and Lincoln lived out is rather different from the hope that our society usually talks about—the kind that we can conjure based on what we

see or read or think, hope held in the bondage of self and circumstance, of political chance or economic vagary. The hope that Peter
spoke of is a hope based on a transcendent source, a God who loves
us and who has been and even now is active in our lives, in this community, in the world. That is the kind of hope that is in us. It enables
us to live out our present vocation unencumbered by all the yester-
days. And it inspires us to see the future as a time of opportunity and
service, as co-workers in God's continuing work of creation.

So great a hope as this is ours—a hope that Peter said we should
be prepared to defend to anyone who asks us to account for it. And
such a defense should be made with gentleness, reverence, and a
clear conscience. All of this assumes we are involved, that we've
joined the creative and redeeming action God has begun on this
earth. That makes us unusual, very different people—different in
what we believe and how we see the world; different in how we act,
seeking to do good and be just; and different in how we feel, showing empathy for those who hurt, guilt when we transgress the will of
a loving God, indignation when injustice occurs, and graciousness
when love is received.

And people "out there" will see such differences in us and they
will ask, "What makes them different? Why are they optimistic, even
idealistic and involved in the face of the wreckage of this world?"
And when people ask such questions of themselves or of us, we need
to be ready with the answers. Be able to answer them, be prepared
to make a defense, advised Peter. In the days of the early church the
learned people of the day—Romans, Jews, and Greeks—all placed
a high priority on the ability to engage in reasoned discourse. That
doesn't imply that you will be able to talk someone into faith but that
your ability to explain the hope that is in you will provide a helpful
witness to them.

The second piece of advice from Peter is that we should give
our accounting with gentleness. A humble and sensitive witness will
bear much more fruit than an arrogant, belligerent, or dogmatic
one. Peter also suggested that we explain the hope that is in us with

reverence. All too easily discussions even within the Christian family can turn sour and acrimonious, and the point of the dialogue is lost in hurt feelings. Having reverence for God and for one another is a way of living out the hope to which we are pointing. Peter's final words are that we should act in such a way as to keep a clear conscience. There is no more powerful witness to our unique hope than a life that bespeaks compassion and character.

The hope that is in us is unique. It breaks all of the boundaries of humankind and it will sustain us in the face of disappointment and, in the end, death itself. To such hope let us make our witness with a clear voice, a gentle spirit, a reverent heart, and a clear conscience.

Amen

Truth and Freedom

John 8:31-36

I have approached these verses from John in the past and have usually backed away from them because the focus of the text on truth and freedom, two words that are both very promising and intimidating. We invoke these words in benediction of many activities. As a college we believe in "the search for truth," wherever it may be found. As a college, we speak of the liberal arts as a means of freeing people from ignorance and equipping them for a meaningful life. As individuals we are concerned about our rights and our freedoms; we want to know "the truth" when our politicians speak to us or when salesmen try to sell us their products.

Truth and freedom are profound words and much of life evolves around the search for, and exercise of, truth and freedom. But Jesus put both of these words in the same sentence when he said, "If you continue in my word, you are truly my disciples, and you will know the truth, and the truth will make you free" (John 8:32). In trying to understand what Jesus meant, let's take the word *freedom* first. We use that word in a lot of different ways and it may be a good idea to consider how we use it before talking about what Christ meant by it, because sometimes our use of the word may get in the way of what Christ had in mind.

First of all, when we speak of freedom it is often in the context of political freedom. Freedom of speech, freedom of the press, and freedom of assembly are important to our social order and not to be taken for granted. We think we know what it means until a purveyor of pornographic images asserts one of these key rights in defense of his or her malevolent deeds. In this text from John the Jews reacted to Christ's description of freedom in terms of political freedom. That's what was on their minds. They pointed out to Jesus that as descendants of Abraham, they had never known bondage. They were free people, not slaves. So in light of their thinking and experience, they asked him, "What do you mean by saying, 'You will be made free'?" (John 8:33). Jesus was talking about something different than political freedom or freedom from tyranny and oppression. Jesus didn't tell them and he doesn't tell us that political freedom is unimportant, just that the freedom he brings is much more significant.

We also talk of freedom in the context of personal rights—the right to associate with whomever we will, to go our own way, to set our own course. In its extreme philosophical form, French philosopher Jean Paul Sartre argued that our freedom is total, unhampered by human circumstance or divine imperative. We can do just what we will and when we will. It means we can assert our individual rights as over against the whole community. German Lutheran scholar and preacher Helmut Thieleke pointed out that this freedom tends to become desperate and often manifests itself in anxiety rather than joy and liberation. We discover that our lives are finite and that unfettered and unguided freedom becomes not a gift but a burden, not an opportunity but a temptation. Driven by whatever urge is strongest, we may discover that we are enslaved and our freedom is gone: the alcoholic is enslaved by increasingly hard to get bottled highs; the liar is in bondage to the need for almost constant deception; the social manipulator is bound by the need for status; and the thief is enslaved to the fruits of another person's labor. Or the bondage may take another form when, defeated by unfettered personal freedom, we look for relief to commanders and commandments, to easy sounding formulas for peace or security or success. Then we become bound to someone else's whim and the stupefying role of automaton.

Personal and political freedom are much heralded in our day, and our understanding of them may introduce some confusion as we consider Christ's words, "You will know the truth, and the truth will make you free." What was Jesus talking about in statements like this one, on a subject we have named after him—Christian freedom? Let's start with the key word, truth. If it is truth that sets us free, what is truth? The truth is that Jesus came to reconcile us to himself. He came to free us from the bondages to which, inevitably, unfettered personal freedom will lead us. And he came to free us from the limitations of political freedom. The truth is, that without calling in the accounts receivable on past sins or present condition, we are called to be God's own. And the truth is, having been reconciled to God, we are free (there's that word again) to serve by being reconcilers to ourselves, to one another, and to the world around us.

These notions of truth and freedom have profound implications for a college that invokes Christ's name. "If you continue in my word" implies attention, study, and discipline. To say that Christ is the truth that frees us is to say that God loves us and the world God created. God wants us here, wishes us well here, wants us to be in harmony with Christ, with one another, and with the world. And so as learners we can explore and enjoy the wonders of this world. And learning becomes an experience of joy and celebration. The library and the laboratory are places of discovery about what God has created for us. Friends and teachers are sources of discovery about ourselves. We can laugh and sing together in celebration of life and the world and experience the joy of being in community.

To say that Christ is the truth that frees us is to identify a primary resource in addressing the central questions of life: questions of meaning, purpose, vocation, relationship, and lifestyle. Christ is Lord of all and his lordship is loving, sympathetic, and affirming. At Concordia we may bring the truth of Christ the reconciler to bear on all of the disciplines and on all of the great questions of justice and peace. To say that Christ is the truth also says that we are free to pass the reconciliation along. We do that as we live out our life on campus, as we help the sick, cheer the friendless, bring joy to those around us, and assume responsibility for the common good.

We pass the reconciliation along as we prepare for future service in times and places yet unseen and unknown. We do it as we move into new fields of study in order to acquire both breadth and depth of understanding so that we can be reconcilers in a variety of stations whether as a service station attendant healing old cars, as a teacher opening the doors to self-realization, or as a corporate lawyer exercising the stewardship of law and wealth.

In the context of our college mission statement, it would be correct to say that the purpose of Concordia is to reconcile the world by sending into society men and women freed by God's grace. In attempting to explain his position on freedom, Jesus told the Jews in the text that "If the Son makes you free, you will be free indeed" (John 8:36). Thanks be to God for this profound truth and freedom, this source of infinite joy and wonder.

Amen

Reconciliation

2 Corinthians 5:16-21

Imagine the stories behind the headlines of almost any daily paper. Parents lose their son in a tragic accident; their dreams shattered, their grief is "irreconcilable." Arab nations and Israel continue to confront each other by resolution and acts of violence. International guarantees and truces are never of more than temporary value because the differences are irreconcilable. A couple divorces after long years of what can only be described as irreconcilable differences. A church goes through conflict and struggle on issues of polity and interpretation. After years of struggle and prayer, some break away from the church body because they discover that their differences are simply irreconcilable.

All around us in families, within ourselves, among nations, and within and among churches, there are irreconcilable differences—people against themselves, against society, against the family, and people against God. These are simply modern versions of the fall as described in Genesis; Adam stood against God and became alienated from Eve and from nature, and finally attempts to flee from God. Fundamentally, each of these actions reflects alienation from God, and in turn alienation from our brothers and sisters as we deny Christ's injunction and God's command to care for others.

Is that all there is to it? That we live in a world of irreconcilable differences? No, of course not. We would not be sharing this time and message if that's all there was to it. There is more to it than that because we know the reconciler, Christ, and we have been given his ministry of reconciliation. But before we consider that ministry, let's reflect on some of the conventional means of dealing with irreconcilable differences. The law is one of our standard responses. It is the basis for determining guilt or innocence; it is the basis for building conformity without which we could not have community. Think of the role of the Ten Commandments in creating and sustaining the Jewish nation. Think about the role of certain rules in sustaining the early Christian communities established by the apostle Paul. A father and mother can, with force and energy, keep order in a family household with appropriate rules and effective discipline. Paul and Luther said that was necessary. But if all there is in the family is the law and its effective enforcement—don't expect a loving, reconciling, affirming relationship. In the book of Matthew we read the story of the young man who asked, "Teacher, what good deed must I do to have eternal life?" (Matt. 19:16). He told Jesus that he kept all of the commandments. Then Jesus told him to sell his belongings and give the proceeds away. And when the young man turned away in sorrow, the disciples asked who could be saved and Jesus said, "For mortals it is impossible" (Matt. 19:26). That is, these acts of righteousness, of law keeping—even that is not enough to reconcile man and God.

Luther saw the law as an instrument of salvation in that it convicts us of sin and drives us to God. He also saw it as useful in providing guidance to the Christian life. But he spoke very sharply about the inappropriateness of the law in reconciling man to God. It was as over against the concept of the works of the law that Luther spoke of faith, grace, and the Word alone. The limits of the law were forcefully stated by Paul when he said, "Now it is evident that no one is justified before God by the law" (Gal. 3:11).

Another of our approaches to reconciliation is through knowledge. Now, far be it for an educator to debunk learning. Indeed, from God's earliest revelation until now he has made himself and his creation knowable, and in some generations God's people have given their best to the study of his revelation. The scholars of the church have provided us with new understandings regarding the Bible. They have raised our consciousness regarding the implications of faith for daily life. Study groups in our churches and on our campus have brought new richness to life and faith for many. Likewise, the fruits of secular study and scholarship are all around us. Today we live longer than ever, we have better homes and cars and food than ever before. We are able to make life more comfortable for those in need and more promising for those in disadvantage. We can and should rejoice in all of that. I believe that God made himself and creation knowable for a purpose, and it is our reasonable service to study, to be faithful students and creative and diligent teachers and scholars.

But our quest for understanding is not unassailable. In eighteenth-century Germany following the thirty years war, moral standards were weak and it was apparent among the peasants, the nobility, and the church leaders. Theologian August Herman Francke spoke out and said the reason for the problem was that religion had become intellectualized and had abandoned its moral dimension. The limits of knowledge in the quest for reconciliation were acknowledged by Luther when he said in his explanation of the Third Article: "I believe that by my own reason or strength I cannot believe in Jesus Christ, my Lord, or come to him."[1] He recognized that there is something of the miraculous in the act of grace; it is something that comes without our doing and without our understanding. Luther was a scholar, a man of profound understanding, both before and after he wrote those words. If we are to be reconciled to God, it must come from outside of ourselves. And if we are to become agents of reconciliation, it requires more than an act of human intelligence or understanding.

We also approach reconciliation through the use of power— economic, political and social power. This is not to be ignored. Think of where the civil rights movement of the 1960s and the women's rights movement of the 1970s would have been without the exercise of power. Sydney Ahlstrom, esteemed Yale historian, writes of the impressive way in which early German pietists used their economic power to establish hospitals, schools and social service agencies to help those in need. Luther spoke of the potentially redemptive role of what he called the secular order as a vehicle of service and love for Christians to their neighbors. And yet, without an abiding and illuminating spirit, power can be misdirected by well meaning people. God has given us power of many kinds and we are expected to use it. And yet, as the single dynamic of reconciliation, it fails. Without changed hearts, the civil rights movement will flounder and the women's movement will not achieve its objectives. We have and should use political influence to insure human rights and justice but always remember that until hearts are changed, the injustice will persist and reconciliation will remain out of our grasp.

So having considered the limitations of the law, knowledge, and power—three of the conventional, essential, and even ordained means of reconciliation—where shall we turn? Into this reality breaks the message of the day, the message of Christ the reconciler. "If anyone is in Christ, there is a new creation: everything old has passed away; see, everything has become new! All this is from God, who reconciled us to himself through Christ . . . reconciling the world to himself, not counting their trespasses against them" (2 Cor. 5:17-19). The first word is that through Christ's action we have been reconciled to God. That's the first priority, reconciliation with God. Without it, we might continue to seek righteousness through power or law or knowledge and end up empty-handed. And Christ offers it to us as a gift! It is his act of grace. "Here it's yours, free!" he says. It doesn't matter if you kept your church pledge, how much money you make, who your colleagues are, how much you know, how much you study. It doesn't matter if you are a liberal or a conservative, it doesn't matter what your theological presuppositions are, it doesn't matter what your current relationship is to your wife, your room-mate, your boss, or your pastor. None of this matters because His act was grace, unconditional grace, and because of that we are literally "new creations."

And the second word is that, having become new creations, we are enabled to be ministers of reconciliation. The text says that the message of reconciliation has been entrusted to us, "So we are ambassadors for Christ, since God is making his appeal through us" (2 Cor. 5:20). Thus, we can become agents of reconciliation to ourselves, our neighbors, our world—to knowledge, to power, and to law and order. And that is possible because the reconciled are not alone; God's Spirit is at work in and through us.

I knew a group of students who broke a certain rule and they expected to be treated with harshness and force. While they did not escape the bite of the law, they were treated with love and respect. That group of people responded to that act of grace with grace. They became ambassadors of the act they had received. That is just a dim image of what God has done for us, and what we are enabled to do as a consequence. This picture of the Israelites from Micah is powerful: "They shall beat their swords into plowshares, and their spears into pruning hooks; nation shall not lift up sword against nation, neither shall they learn war any more; but they shall all sit under their own vines and under their own fig trees, and no one shall make them afraid; for the mouth of the Lord of hosts has spoken" (Micah 4:3-4).

Reconcilers are not called to easy tasks in their ministry in the world. Alvin Rogness, former president of Luther Seminary, put it this way: "We are not to anchor our lives in some sheltered cove and let the storm-tossed world go by. The Lord's call is not like that. Not to an easier task but a greater cause. Not to peace but to battle. Not to a cozy harbor but to the sea of storms. We are not built for safe harbors. We are built for storms."[2] We are called to consider the conventional means of reconciliation and call them by their names: that power doesn't impress God; that knowledge without faith and mystery is hollow; that law and order without grace can only string a person out, not make him or her whole. In addition, as ministers of reconciliation we can speak the affirming word, the word of grace.

Many of you are aware that my academic background is in speech communication—so you will recognize my emphasis on the importance of words. While we communicate with more than words, psychologists tell us that they can see inside a person by listening to the pattern of his or her words. Child development experts tell us that young children think of themselves, in large part, in terms of the words that people use to describe them and nurture them. I think that reconciliation occurs when the affirming word is the word that characterizes our vocabulary. Paul's words to the Ephesians are among my favorites:

> Do not use harmful words, but only helpful words, the kind that build up and provide what is needed, so that what you say will do good to those who hear you. And do not make God's Holy Spirit sad; for the Spirit is God's mark of ownership on you, a guarantee that the Day will come when God will set you free. Get rid of all bitterness, passion, and anger. No more shouting or insults, no more hateful feelings of any sort. Instead, be kind and tender-hearted to one another, and forgive one another, as God has forgiven you through Christ. (Eph. 4:29-32)[3]

In addition, we are called to be reconcilers in our careers. Luther put it this way:

> If you are a manual laborer you find that the Bible has been put into your workshop, into your hand, into your heart. It teaches and preaches how you should treat your neighbor. Just look at your tools—at your needle or thimble, your beer barrel, your goods, your scales or yardstick or measure—and you read this statement inscribed on them. . . "Friend, use me in your relations with your neighbor just as you would want your neighbor to use his property in his relations with you."[4]

Christ came that we might have life and have it abundantly. He took the first step—defying the rules of law, of knowledge, and of power. He took that step because he loved us and wanted us to be reconciled to him. He introduced a new dynamic into life, the dynamic of grace. And the ultimate result of his reconciliation comes to us in these words from Revelation 21:3-4: "See, the home of God is among mortals. He will dwell with them as their God; they will be his peoples, and God himself will be with them; he will wipe every tear from their eyes. Death will be no more; mourning and crying and pain will be no more, for the first things have passed away."

These are the promises of Christ the reconciler and because of them; we shall live and through us, our neighbors too.

Amen

Vocation

Philippians 2:1-8

The most frequent and well-intentioned question seniors hear in the closing days of their college career is this: "What are your plans for next year?" And the answer people expect will have to do with career, with job, with profession. The question is good and helpful, one I frequently ask. Today I wish to push the envelope on that question by talking about vocation. Vocation is a larger conceptual category than what we usually have in mind when we ask someone what they plan to do next year.

Vocatio is a Latin word. It means "a summons, a calling." This is going to be an autobiographical telling as I share with you how I have come to understand vocation. Let me begin by identifying the sources of my understanding. The first and foremost source is my faith. The best expression of the way in which my faith shapes my understanding of vocation is in these words from Luther's explanation of the Second Article:

> I believe that Jesus Christ, true God, begotten of the Father from eternity, and also true man, born of the Virgin Mary, is my Lord, who has redeemed me, a lost and condemned creature, delivered me and freed me from all sins, from death, and from the power of the devil, not with silver and gold but with his holy and precious blood and with his innocent sufferings and death, in order that I might be his, live under him in his kingdom, and serve him in everlasting righteousness, innocence, and blessedness, even as he has risen from the dead and lives and reigns to all eternity. This is most certainly true.[1]

These words affirm my conviction about my nature—fallen and without capacity for perfection in the eyes of God. They also affirm my conviction that God has freed me from the bondage of my nature, my irresponsibility. God has done everything that is necessary for my salvation in Christ. And, in consequence, I have been called and enabled to serve God. In other words, by the grace of God faith can become active in my life. God has called me to do that not to earn my salvation but to live out the praise, the gratitude, that is in my soul.

A second source of my understanding of vocation is found in the writings of Martin Luther. Indeed, most Christian denominations acknowledge a debt of gratitude for Luther's thoughtfulness about these matters. When Luther lived, the idea of vocation or calling was restricted to those who held such churchly offices as monk, priest, or nun. Other Christians, peasants and professionals alike, were excluded. Luther turned all of that on its ear. In his famous essay on "The Freedom of a Christian," he referred to Philippians 2:4-7 in which Paul wrote:

> Let each of you look not to your own interests, but to the interests of others. Let the same mind be in you that was in Christ Jesus, who, though he was in the form of God, did not regard equality with God as something to be exploited, but emptied himself, taking the form of a slave, being born in human likeness.

Luther went on in his writings to expand the boundaries of our understanding of who was called. We are all called he said. Likewise, he expanded the idea of what we are called to do. Luther said that we are to be Christ to people in every place imaginable. His was a holistic view of vocation, of servant life, before it became part of any popular lexicon. He spoke of service in marriage, in the family, in the community, in the church, in public life, in our active years, and in our retirement. And his blessing of careers was inclusive of teachers, dressmakers, street sweepers, brewers, housekeepers, farmers—all careers that were laudable and constructive of life. A church document some years ago reinforced un understanding of ministry as work that cannot be limited to certain persons, places, and times, because ministry is God's activity in the lives of God's people for the life of the world *in every time and place.*

A third source of my understanding of vocation is the example of my father, a straightforward farmer for most of his eighty-two years. Now I must say of my father as Mark Twain did about his, the longer I lived, the wiser he became. And so it continues. My father was very attentive to the needs of the extended family. He took time, he supported and encouraged, he disciplined and advised. This was very difficult at times, particularly in the depression years through which he lived out the best years of his life. I was always impressed by my dad's high standards of stewardship as a farmer. The fact that his rows and furrows were the straightest in the neighborhood was a matter of good stewardship and not neighborly competition. And he was always attending to the latest developments in crop varieties, conservation measures, and soil care. He was a man of the community, especially the church and the township. I was almost always first in my class in the weekly current events tests in our school because at home we heard the news, read the news, and talked the news. The affairs of the world were on our family agenda. Dad was not a man of words; he never talked to me about his calling or his vocation. But I have come to understand that his life was his most eloquent statement.

If these are the sources of my understanding of vocation, then what have I come to understand about it? First, there is equality among vocations and callings. There are many places and vocations for service and one is not elevated above the other. Now we are tempted by secular standards to do just that. But that is not what the tradition tells us. The worldly status that we confer on a professor over a student or a lawyer over a laborer is entirely inconsistent with the biblical tradition and the confessional writings of the church.

I have also come to understand something about excellence. Once when Luther was responding to a question about the quality of public leadership he said he would rather be ruled by a wise Turk than a foolish Christian. Luther was reflecting the biblical injunction to care for the neighbor. We don't all have the same gifts, but we are expected to do the very best we can with the gifts we have been given. Piety is never an excuse for mediocrity.

And there is another piece here: we don't have to be perfect. First of all, it is not in our nature, and best of all, God doesn't expect it. But as grateful servants we surely are called to do our best for the sake of the neighbor. British author and scholar Dorothy L. Sayers said, "The only Christian work is good work well done."[2] Understood this way, work is not primarily a thing one does to live—a means to making a living—but the thing one lives to do—a calling; a vocation.

I have also come to understand something about discipline in thinking about my vocation. Luther said that in God's kingdom, grace reigns, and we can be sure of that. But in the world, the law reigns, and we ignore that at our peril. For example, when an accountant makes a million dollar error in computing the financial condition of a company or a physician makes a wrong diagnosis, the error has concrete consequences that cannot be erased or reversed. Or, when a parent neglects a family, the children suffer, and the sins of the fathers and the mothers are passed on to the children and the grandchildren. And here at Concordia, the college's books must be balanced and the equipment and buildings kept in good repair or the mission and quality of what we are about will be compromised.

For most of us, vocation is collaborative; that is, our calling often involves working with people whose political views or moral values or religious faith may be different from our own. But Luther encouraged us to work with people on behalf of justice and the common good. We are not to isolate ourselves as individual servants or as a servant church or as a College in mission. Rather, we are to look for fruitful partnerships.

Vocation is also about crosses we may encounter in life, such as in our career when our company is downsized or with our children when a parent leaves the family or to a retired person whose savings are squandered by an incompetent money manager. And there are crosses we build ourselves due to our lack of diligence or self-discipline. The law of God helps us see such crosses. Whether crosses find us or we build them ourselves, they are occasions of suffering and regret, but also of grace when God's redeeming Spirit comes into our lives.

Vocation is also about renewal—spiritual renewal—that comes as we experience God's grace and nurture the love that God has placed in our lives. Renewal is essential to my vocation. If I am to live the life of praise with my family, colleagues and friends, I better give time to nurture such a life. And if I am to stay sharp and effective in the complex, demanding, and graceless world in which I live and serve, I had better renew my skills on a regular basis.

There is more to my biography on vocation than I have shared, and by God's grace, I will surely come to know more. When my father was in his final illness, I sat with him one morning as he lay between sleep and wakefulness. He was not aware of my presence. He reached back into the legacy of his life and recited these words:

> I believe that God has created me and all that exists; that he has given and still sustains my body and soul, all my limbs and senses, my reason and all the faculties of my mind, together with food and clothing, house and home, family and property; that he provides me daily and abundantly with all the necessities of life, protects me from all danger, and preserves me from all evil. All this he does out of his pure, fatherly, and divine goodness and mercy, without any merit or worthiness on my part. For all of this I am bound to thank, praise, serve, and obey Him. This is most certainly true.[3]

Amen

Refuge

Luke 13:31-35; Philippians 3:17-4:7

I grew up on a farm in Minnesota. We had chickens on the farm, hens that would make nests, lay their eggs, and sit on them until they hatched. As a child, I was impatient about waiting out the hatch. My mother told me I must not disturb the sitting hen or she would abandon her eggs. And eventually the eggs would hatch, usually resulting in eight to ten yellow balls of feather. These chicks were extremely helpless, entirely dependent and very vulnerable.

The chicks had many natural enemies—predator cats and weasels and foxes too. Often, all that would stand between the chicks and their predator was the guile of the mother hen who kept the chicks in settled areas where foxes and their kind could be seen. They also protected the chicks with their cackle and cluck, and the shelter of their wings under which the chicks could gather. In the natural order of things, if two-thirds of the chicks survived, it was very good; if half survived, it was all right. Occasionally, however, the mother hen would lose all of her chicks.

Our gospel text from Luke 13 is about foxes and hens and chicks. One of the wonderful things about Jesus' ministry was his use of so many familiar images in telling his story: fishes and loaves, vine and branches, mustards and fig trees, and all the rest. But this is no prosaic tale of animal life; it is a parable that talks about the fate of the human soul. In the text Herod is the fox, a predator seeking to control and take and devour. Jesus is the hen who seeks to protect at all costs the ones he loves. And the people—the sick, the anxious, the outcast, the vulnerable, the confused, the seekers—they are the chicks. This is no fairytale where the fox and the hen become friends; the chicken does not end up lying down with the fox. In this story the hen—Jesus—is killed and the vulnerable ones are left to fend for themselves. Many do not survive. So the fox ends up winning, right? Well, stay tuned until the end of the story.

There is much to ponder here, so let's go back to the beginning. Let's take some more time to understand the fox. Herod's first priority was self-preservation and his second priority was the preservation of the empire. He was not a friendly sort of fellow. He did what he needed to do to survive. He killed off family members who threatened him. He had John the Baptist beheaded to keep a favored guest happy. He was worked up about Jesus. And why was this? Because the eastern flank of the Roman Empire for which he was responsible was vulnerable. His job was to maintain a balance between the aspirations of the empire and the expectations of the temple-worshiping Israelites. So he could not afford to take any risks with a guy from the country—from left field, if you will—who might upset the balance. So in trying to take Jesus out by whatever means, this sly, cunning fox Herod was just doing his job.

Are there any Herods, any foxes, in your town? In my town? In my country? And what would that fox look like? Would he look like some of the folks that the apostle Paul was concerned about in his letter to the Philippians? Paul was worried that the people he had loved and to whom he had ministered were vulnerable to the siren songs of many attractive, seemingly friendly foxes—folks who preached the gospel of self-indulgence and self-dependence, of gluttony and debauchery. Or would the fox look like some of the folks Paul found in the church at Corinth? They had heard Paul preach but then they divided themselves into sects, sects built around the personality cults of Cephas and Appollos and Jesus. They became so self-absorbed that they forgot all about Jesus, about loving God and neighbor, about a community in Christ that is forgiving and without ego.

Or would the modern day fox look like the former president of Haiti who betrayed the promise of his early religious calling by surrounding himself with luxury, profiting from corruption and ignoring the elemental needs of a trusting nation. Would the modern Herod, that old fox, be found among us? Would Herod be found among those who cry for tax relief in the face of want and a massive public debt, who pillage our investment accounts with insider trading, platinum parachutes, and creative accounting? I submit that the Herods, the foxes, also find ways to infiltrate our churches today as they did in Paul's time. Feeling good has too often replaced being good, and therapy too often replaces confession and accountability. In modern times even many religious leaders eschew the legitimate place of values and discipline for fear of being labeled "legalists." And there are the stealth foxes who would transform our wants into needs, who convert us from servers to users, who subtly move us from neighbor to self, from justice to juice, from Jesus to just us. Those foxes may be harder to identify but they are no less real than Herod.

From the foxes we move to the chicks. Jesus gave us clear examples of who in his mind were the chicks. They were the vulnerable, those who languished in poverty, the sick for whom no one would provide proper care, the people who couldn't reach the healing waters, those who were blind from birth, the person with the untreated blood disease. They were the people who were confused, like the wealthy farmer who wasn't sure what really mattered in his life or the scribes and Pharisees who confused religious conformity with salvation. The chicks included the outcasts; the demon possessed who wondered the streets and fields, the women of the street who hustled their bodies to stay alive, and the sinners whose life stories would surpass any of the reality shows on television these days. And the seekers were among the chicks too—people like Zacchaeus the wealthy tax collector who was not satisfied and Thomas who kept asking questions.

What about the chicks in our town and time and place? There are the vulnerable around and among us. We find them in homeless shelters and among those running out of welfare eligibility or living without health insurance. There are vulnerable chicks in America, the world's wealthiest nation, where twenty percent of our citizens live in poverty. And there are vulnerable people in a world where three quarters of our four billion people are poor, one quarter live in absolute poverty, and ten million—most of whom are children—die from malnutrition. You know the vulnerable in your neighborhood; you can put a face on the perpetually unemployed, those chemically dependent, people caught in a web of despair, victims of betrayal and abandonment, those who face death, people without hope.

We find people in confusion in our neighborhoods too. Recall the text from Philippians 3. Paul found in Philippi people confused by the siren sounds of false prophets. And their fate? Paul put it straight when he wrote, "Their end is destruction; their god is the belly; and their glory is in their shame; their minds are set on earthly things" (Phil. 3:19). It is so easy to fall for the gods of cheap pleasure, of easy virtue, of the quick fix and the easy answer. The outcasts are among us too. We think of those who are imprisoned and terrorized by religious and political fanatics. Think as well of those who by virtue of skin color or gender of place of birth are shut out from opportunity and respectability and justice. And as in Jerusalem, there are seekers in our towns. Lutheran theologian Marva Dawn says that people around us, now more than ever, are looking for a story that will give meaning for their lives. Authorities tell us that the rising generation is looking for sterner stuff than the pop culture. Indeed, they are more likely than their parents to read the Bible, to go to church and to pray. Seekers, seekers all, chicks scratching and scrambling to find safety, security, and salvation from the foxes.

We've looked at the fox and the chicks. Now it is time to consider the mother hen. It's clear from the text that Jesus saw himself as the mother hen, and he was intent on looking out for his flock. Even when he was warned that death awaited him if he persisted in his ministry of caring for vulnerable, seeking, and confused chicks, he would not be deterred. That fox Herod would not keep him from exorcising demons and healing the sick, he said plainly and he meant what he said! Jesus placed the chicks first on his list of priorities. Barbara Brown Taylor, a wonderful preacher and writer, describes the hen standing between the chicks and the fox. There she is without fangs or claws or rippling muscles—simply holding out her wings so that she may gather and protect and love the vulnerable, the confused, the outcast, and the seeking chicks. The fox sees that he will have to kill her to get the chicks and he does. "It breaks her heart, but it does not change a thing. If you mean what you say, then this is how you stand," writes Taylor. And so Jesus became vulnerable for us and died in the process because he meant what he said. And he wept—he wept for the souls who wouldn't come to him. "If you have ever loved someone you could not protect, then you understand the depth of Jesus' lament."[1] So "Jerusalem, Jerusalem" Jesus cried out in despair (Luke 13:34).

The story of the chicks and the fox and the mother hen does not end there. God would not let it end there. So God raised Jesus from the dead. And God sent his Spirit so that love and care would abide and people like you and I could continue the practices of a mother hen by being role models to the young, by providing support for the weary and sick, by working in the community for the common good, by reaching across the nation and across the globe to feed and heal and sustain vulnerable chicks. Yes, Jesus lives through us and because he lives, the foxes will not have the last word. Christ empowers us to gather his chicks even as he gathers us.

And so God's kingdom will surely come. And blessed is he who comes in the name of the Lord.

Amen

Grace

Exodus 34:5-9; Luke 19:1-10

When our son was fifteen he joined his church group for a winter evening on the Fargo dike. In the flatlands of the Red River Valley, the dike offered a change in topography sufficient to challenge a tobogganer, a sledder, or a skier. Our son decided to descend the slope on an inner tube, standing up and going backward. The result, a broken leg, was to be expected. (By the way, our son never asked for our sympathy after the mishap.) The story reminds me of my days as a teacher. When a student did sloppy work that was often late, it was not unexpected that the student receive a C or a D for the term. Now use your imagination a bit in an entirely different context. You're fishing for rainbow trout in a lake. Such a quest requires quite specialized rigging and bait. But let's say that instead of catching a trout you snag a walleye. Now that would be unexpected.

The biblical texts from Exodus and Luke are not about such mundane matters as sledding or teaching or catching fish, but they are about both "the expected" and the "unexpected." In the lesson from Exodus there is a strong word about what we can expect from God if we ignore him or defy him: he will visit the iniquity of the fathers upon the children and the children's children onto the third and fourth generations. Those are heavy words. Lutherans have a tradition of thinking about God's law in a couple of different ways. The first use of the law is to help us order life in the world. We believe there are basic rules of living that we should obey, and if we don't, we should expect to pay the consequences. Defy the rule of gravity and jump off a ten-story building, and—saint or sinner—you can expect a "bad hurt" when you hit the ground. Treat your neighbors with disrespect and insults and you can expect a chilly neighborhood. And further, conduct your life in a self-indulgent, immoral way and you can expect to pay the consequences in a life that is meager at best or destructive at worst. This use of the law has nothing to do with God's mercy. God loves you, saint or sinner, but you and I cannot expect that God will spare us from the harmful consequences of our misdeeds and, indeed, we can expect that the iniquities of the fathers will be visited upon the children to the third and fourth generation.

Think of what happens in a society that ignores these expectations about which God has forewarned us. We live in a land of plenty, where, we increasingly focus on the pursuit of individual happiness that is often unencumbered by moral precept or religious inhibition. We live in a land where violence and pornography flood the media—movies, DVDs, CDs, and all the rest—while scholars have established a definite link between exposure to such material and human conduct. We live in a land of limited resources, yet we squander our natural inheritance as if there were no tomorrow. And what shall we expect from such behavior? Look at the statistics on child abuse, on poverty rates, on incarceration, on violent crime, on white-collar crime, on loan foreclosures, and on global warming.

How did all of this occur? Some say that the family is to blame for not cultivating virtue and self-control in their children. Others blame the schools for shying away from values in the name of the separation of church and state. Still others blame the church for getting so caught up in secular society that it forgot its own foundations. Some observers blame social engineering that promoted justice without reference to conduct and character. And still others say it's because of bad practices in the financial industry. However you assess the causes, about this there is no doubt: the iniquities of the fathers and the mothers are being visited upon the third and fourth generations. And for those who know the Exodus story and recite the confessions of the church and hear the word preached in its truth and purity, there should be no surprise in any of this—it is entirely expected.

But these biblical texts do not end with what we may expect. The life-giving word in the Gospel from Luke 19 is all about the unexpected. There is, first of all, this Zacchaeus whom we meet in this text that has been described as the symbol and summation of Luke's Jesus. Zacchaeus was a publican, a tax collector who collaborated with the despised Romans. Jericho was his town and it was a wealthy town of commerce. Tax collectors did all right financially so Zacchaeus probably lacked no material comforts, and as a public official, he was treated with deference. In many ways it would be fair to say in the parlance of our day that Zacchaeus "had it made." But on the other hand, we are also told that he was short of stature, conjuring the image of a man who always had to struggle for attention and perhaps respect. And Zacchaeus was not at peace. Something was missing. Perhaps it was a family crisis; a son gone bad or a daughter run away. Or had Zacchaeus defrauded someone? We don't know why this outwardly successful man was anxious, but it was quite unexpected. And it was also surprising that someone like him would join the crowd who had come to meet Jesus, for he was unlike them, his presence was very much unexpected.

Another surprising aspect of the text comes when Jesus recognized Zacchaeus. You know the story, short man that he was, Zacchaeus ran ahead of the crowd and climbed a tree so that he would have a good vantage point when Jesus came walking by. Imagine, this dignified man of status climbing up a tree—unexpected indeed! As Zacchaeus sat in a tree, he set the stage for the next unexpected event: Jesus not only recognized him but instructed him to come down because he was going to come to his house for dinner. This unexpected invitation scandalized the Pharisees. Jesus, they said, has no standards. He calls upon an outcast, an opportunist—nay an oppressor—and ignores us, the holy high order of Jericho. Unexpected, entirely unexpected.

Or was it? If they had been following Jesus' ministry they would have known he had already eaten with a rich man, he had been baptized by a social misfit, he had ministered to a Samaritan woman, and he had called a publican and a zealot to join his ministry. I mean this Jesus was always doing the unexpected. And he was, after all, the Son of God, a God who throughout history had taken an unexpected interest in some strange folks, like Moses the murderer, Abraham the liar, Jacob the thief, Rahab the harlot, Ruth the woman of Moab, and David the adulterer. Jesus was an outsider and he identified with outsiders, people in need were just the ones he was looking for, even the very least.

A third surprise in this text comes with the transformation of Zacchaeus. Jesus reached out to Zacchaeus in his need and he was changed completely. Half his goods would go to the poor, not the tithe called for by the religious establishment. And anyone whom he had defrauded would be restored fourfold. This was not "tit for tat" works righteousness; this was a voluntary response to Christ's gift. And how did the story end? With Jesus words: "Today salvation has come to this house, because he too is a son of Abraham. For the Son of Man came to seek out and to save the lost" (Luke 19:9-10).

The good news that throbs throughout the texts is that God, who would have every right to punish us for our rebellion, does the unexpected. God comes to us with the grace-full, gospel news of forgiveness. When Moses came down the mountain with God's law in hand only to see that the people were worshipping Baal, he was furious, and in his anger he broke the tablets of stone. God was even more angry, threatening blood. But time passed and God, still recognizing the need of his people for discipline and order and justice, came again to Moses with two new tablets of instruction. And God assured Moses that he would be merciful and gracious, slow to anger and abiding in steadfast love and faithfulness. It was, to say the least, unexpected and undeserved—but such are the ways of God.

If God could come in such unexpected ways to the lost and anxious Zacchaeus and to the rebellious nation of Israel, then why not also to you and me? God is looking for you. Is there an issue in your life that is unresolved, some deep question or doubt or uncertainty? Then God is looking for you. Is there a broken relationship in your life, within your family, with a neighbor or a coworker? God is looking for you. Is there a sin in your life that is persistent, some thorn in the flesh, a restlessness of conscience that will not go away? God is looking for you. This God whom we worship today sent his Son Jesus to find lost people, hurting people, anxious people, guilty people.

And once God finds you, God will transform you in ways that may be surprising. I think of an acquaintance who gives portion of each year to healing people in some of the most destitute and dangerous parts of the world. I think of a successful entrepreneur whose great joy is to create jobs for people who need them. I think of a public servant who believes that prudence and justice are not mutually exclusive. I think of a volunteer who brings comfort to those in the AIDS ward of the hospital. This is the Christ who does not count our trespasses against us, who reconciles us to himself, and who gives us a ministry of reconciliation. You can think of scores of friends and loved ones who have walked in the valley of the shadow. God has found them because God was looking for them, and their lives have been transformed. God has promised to dry our tears, to walk the lonely miles, to stand with us against all who would stand against us.

To end where we began: we should not expect the laws of nature to yield in the face of our self-indulgence or our flagrant violations. In the real world, our sins may indeed be visited upon the third and fourth generations and the evidence is arrayed around us. But we can expect that God will deal graciously with our souls and that God is looking for us even now. And when we look to him, when we climb our sycamore tree in search of his truth and mercy, he will surely find us. And he will be merciful and gracious. That is not unexpected.

Amen

Appendix of Homilies

Faith and Learning

"Faith and Belief," delivered February 1994
"Faith and Community," delivered February 1999
"Faith and Complaint," delivered November 1994
"Faith and Death," delivered February 1995
"Faith and Discipleship," delivered April 2008
"Faith and Doubt," delivered November 1979
"Faith and Honor," delivered January 1990
"Faith and Legacy," delivered February 1988
"Faith and Politics," delivered November 1996
"Faith and Suffering," delivered November 1997
"Faith and Unity," delivered November 1995
"Faith and Wealth," delivered October 1994
"Faith and Work," delivered October 1993

Seasons of Faith

"A Holy Restlessness," Opening Convocation, Fall 2003
"Not So Wild a Dream," Homecoming, Fall 1995
"Salty Days and Starry Nights," Homecoming, Fall 1997
"Life in the Christian Colony," New Semester, Fall 2007
"And the Word Became Flesh," Advent, Winter 1976
"God's Future," Epiphany, Winter 1997
"An Uncomfortable Day," Ash Wednesday, Winter 1987
"Bargaining with God," Lent, Spring 1998

"To Be Continued," Easter, Spring 2004
"Mass of Exodus," End of the Academic Year, Spring 1994
"Apocalypse Now," Pentecost, Fall 1998

Elements of Faith

"Forgiveness," delivered September 2008
"Hope," delivered February 1989
"Truth and Freedom," delivered February 1977
"Reconciliation," delivered January 1979
"Vocation," delivered March 1996
"Refuge," delivered March 2004
"Grace," delivered November 1995

Notes

Faith and Belief

1. Nelson, Hubert, "Deitrich Bonhoeffer" in *Daily Readings from Spiritual Classics,* ed. Paul Ofstedal (Minneapolis: Augsburg Fortress, 1990), 322.

Faith and Community

1. Parker J. Palmer, "A Place Called Community" in *The Christian Century,* March 19, 1977, http://www.religion-online.org/showarticle .asp?title=1143.
2. Ibid.

Faith and Discipleship

1. Alfred Tennyson, edited by Hallam Tennyson, *Idylls of the King: Annotated by Alfred, Lord Tennyson* (London: Macmillan, 1913), 2.
2. C. S. Lewis, *God in the Dock: Essays on Theology and Ethics* (Grand Rapids, Mich.: Eerdmans, 1994), 105.

Faith and Honor

1. Martin Luther, "Ten Commandments," *The Small Catechism* in Theodore G. Tappert, trans. and ed., *The Book of Concord: The Confessions of the Evangelical Lutheran Church* (Philadelphia: Fortress Press, 1959), 343.
2. Robert N. Munsch, illustrated by Sheila McGraw, *Love You Forever* (Logan, Iowa: Perfection Learning, 1987).

bottom

left

right

center

top-left

top-right

bottom-left

bottom-right

top-center

bottom-center

left-center

right-center

center-left

center-right

center-top

center-bottom

center-center

top-top

bottom-bottom

left-left

right-right

top-middle

bottom-middle

left-middle

right-middle

middle

middle-top

middle-bottom

middle-left

middle-right

middle-center

Faith and Politics

1. Concordia's mission statement: *The purpose of Concordia College is to influence the affairs of the world by sending into society thoughtful and informed men and women dedicated to the Christian life.*

2. Reinhold Niebuhr, *Moral Man and Immoral Society: A Study in Ethics and Politics* (New York: Charles Scribner's Sons, 1934), 23.

3. Ibid, 4.

4. Scripture taken from the Good News Translation—Second Edition Copyright © 1992 by American Bible Society. Used by Permission.

Faith and Suffering

1. This homily draws on the insights of Douglas John Hall, which are recorded in *God and Human Suffering: An Exercise in the Theology of the Cross* (Minneapolis: Augsburg Fortress, 1987).

Faith and Unity

1. "Simple Gifts," Elder Joseph Brackett Jr., 1848.

Faith and Wealth

1. Augustine, *The Confessions* (Edinburgh: T & T Clark, 1876), 1.

Faith and Work

1. Soren Kierkegaard, *Soren Kierkegaard's Journals and Papers,* eds. Howard V. and Edna H. Hong (Bloomington, Ind.: Indiana University Press, 1967), 277.

A Holy Restlessness

1. Pope John Paul II, Address to the Fiftieth General Assembly of the United Nations Organization, New York, October 5, 1995. Found at www.vatican.va/holy_father/john_paul_ii/speeches/1995/october/documents/hf_jp-ii_spe_05101995_address-to-uno_en.html.

2. Ibid, emphasis added.

3. This quote is credited to Anain Nin on several websites dedicated to quotations, including www.quotationspage.com, www.brainyquote.com, and www.thinkexist.com.

4. "Hope for Africa," *Newsweek*, July 14, 2003. Found at http://www.newsweek.com/id/57835.

5. William Barclay, *The Daily Study Bible, Vol. 8: The Letter to the Romans* (Philadelphia: Westminster Press, 1958), 231.

6. Sharon Parks, *The Critical Years* (San Francisco: Harper and Row, 1986).

Not So Wild a Dream

1. Gwendolyn Brooks, *In Montgomery and other Poems* (Chicago: The Third World Press, 2003), 57–58.

Salty Days and Starry Nights

1. "In Little Rock, Clinton Warns of Racial Split," *The New York Times*, September 26, 1997. Found at http://www.nytimes.com/1997/09/26/us/in-little-rock-clinton-warns-of-racial-split.html.

2. Michael J. Sandel, *Democracy's Discontent: America in Search of a Public Philosophy* (Cambridge: Harvard University Press, 1996), 3.

3. Anthony B. Robinson, "Practicing Our Faith: A Way of Life for a Searching People," *The Christian Century*, July 16, 1997.

4. James M. Wall, "Moral Center: Deep Faith Likes the Pope—humor—John Paul II Visits the U.S.—Editorial," *The Christian Century*, October 25, 1995.

5. Pope John Paul II, Address to the Fiftieth General Assembly of the United Nations Organization, New York, October 5, 1995. Found at www.vatican.va/holy_father/john_paul_ii/speeches/1995/october/documents/hf_jp-ii_spe_05101995_address-to-uno_en.html.

Life in the Christian Colony

1. Stanley Hauerwas and William H. Willimon, *Resident Aliens: Life in the Christian Colony,* (Abingdon, 1989), 12.

2. Attributed to Josiah Gilbert Holland. Found at www.giga-usa.com/quotes/topics/thought_t007.htm.

And the Word Became Flesh

1. "Lift Up Your Heads, Ye Mighty Gates," George Weissel (1590-1635), trans., Catherine Winkworth (1829-1878).

God's Future

1. Luther E. Smith, from a convocation speech to students at Emory University, Atlanta, Georgia, *Chronicle of Higher Education*, October 11, 1996.

2. Cornelius Plantinga, Jr., *Not the Way It's Supposed to Be: A Breviary of Sin* (Grand Rapids, Mich.: Eerdmans, 1995), 3.

An Uncomfortable Day

1. *Lutheran Book of Worship* (Minneapolis: Augsburg Publishing House, 1978), p. 56.

To Be Continued

1. The Rev. David Simonson suffered a stroke in the spring of 2004. He and his wife Eunice, both Concordia graduates, were awarded the Luther Institute's Wittenberg Award for humanitarianism and witness to faith in November 2004. See http://jimklobucharwrites.com/Archives/Simonson.html.

2. Dru Sjodin, a student at the University of North Dakota in Grand Forks, eighty miles north of Moorhead, was kidnapped, raped, and murdered on November 22, 2003. Her body was recovered April 17, 2004, near Crookston, Minnesota.

3. Martin Luther, "The Lord's Prayer," in *The Book of Concord*, ed. and trans. Theodore G. Tappert (Philadelphia: Fortress Press), 346.

4. *The New Interpreter's Bible*, vol. XI (Nashville: Abingdon, 2000), 395.

5. Martin Luther, "The Lord's Prayer," 347.

6. My first farewell was upon my retirement from Concordia's presidency at the close of the 1998–1989 academic year. I returned to Concordia in 2003 to serve as Interim President for one year.

Apocalypse Now

1. Stephen L. Carter, *Civility* (New York: Harper Perennial, 1998), 78.

2. Ibid. 18.

Hope

1. John F. Kennedy, Inaugural Address, January 20, 1961, www
.bartleby.com/124/pres63.html.

Reconciliation

1. Martin Luther, "The Creed," *The Small Catechism* in Theodore
G. Tappert, trans. and ed., *The Book of Concord: The Confessions of the
Evangelical Lutheran Church* (Philadelphia: Fortress Press, 1959), 345.

2. Alvin Rogness, "Storm Centers," *Captured by Mystery* (Minneapolis, Augsburg, 1966), 43.

3. Scripture taken from the Good News Translation–Second Edition
Copyright © 1992 by American Bible Society. Used by Permission.

4. "The Sermon on the Mount" (1538). *Luther's Works* 21:237 (St.
Louis: Concordia Publishing House, 1956).

Vocation

1. Martin Luther, "The Creed," *The Small Catechism* in Theodore
G. Tappert, trans. and ed., *The Book of Concord: The Confessions of the
Evangelical Lutheran Church* (Philadelphis: Fortress Press, 1959), 345.

2. Dorothy L. Sayers, "Why Work?" An address delivered at East-
bourne on April 23, 1942 (London: Methuen & Co, 1942).

3. Martin Luther, "The Creed," 345.

Refuge

1. Barbara Brown Taylor, "As a Hen Gathers Her Brood" The Christian Century (February 25, 1986): 201. Found at www.religion-online
.org/showarticle.asp?title=638.